on becoming a

PSY-COSMETOLOGIST

Salon Professionals
Who Feel
The Beauty in People

Dr. Lewis Losoncy

© 2013 by People Media Inc.
345 Morgantown Road, Reading, PA 19611

Published by People Media Inc.

This is the 10th edition. Please visit our website at:
www.peoplemedia.com

ISBN 978-0-9894285-0-7

Printed in the United States of America.

On Becoming A Psy-Cosmetologist

To
The Psy-Cosmetologists

Your Artistic Medium is Not a Canvas,
And Will Not Hang in the Louvre;
You Have a Higher, a Human Purpose:
Your Artistry is On People,
Who Come to Life in the Process!

To the Psy-Cosmetologists who touch nearly everyone's life,
I would like to communicate my love and respect for you.
I have learned from you, laughed with you, sang with you, cried
with you, and watched you grow, watched your
professionalism, and watched the world open its eyes and heart
to you. You are the new Psy-Cosmetologist.

"It is my considered opinion that the hairdresser is the most influential person in any community. When the public goes to a hairdresser, something happens to them. They feel safe, they relax. The hairdresser knows what their skin is like under the makeup; they know their age; they don't have to keep up any kind of pretense. People tell a hairdresser things they wouldn't dare confess to a priest and they are open about matters they try to conceal from a doctor. When people place their secret lives in the hairdresser's hands, the hairdresser gains an authority few other people attain. I have heard hairdressers quoted with complete conviction on art, literature, politics, economics, child care and morals. I tell you that a clever, thoughtful, ambitious hairdresser wields a power beyond the comprehension of most people."

– John Steinbeck, *Travels with Charley: In Search of America*

Tears streamed from the well-dressed attorney's eyes as she embraced her attaché case. In the heart of the Phoenix airport, the roar of 727s broke the silence. The stranger was turning her attention from the briefs she was reading to tuning in to our conversation. Finally, she interrupted our conversation.

"When you two first started to talk, I thought that you were exaggerating, overstating the case. I mean, a stylist, or what you call a Psy-Cosmetologist, being important in society? I thought, "What do they do but cut hair? Why the big deal?" And then as you talked about their impact in the neighborhood, even society, it really opened my eyes."

A silence.

"You see, my mother was a stylist, and I guess I never realized the importance of her work on peoples' lives. But now I think of the calls she would get at night to help her customers, I mean clients, for their proms or weddings or whatever, and how she would put ribbons in the little girls' hair, including my own, to give that little extra touch, that extra good feeling.

I never thought about it. I just took her for granted. And yet she has done more for people than I could ever do. I just wish I would have thought about these things before. I wish I could have communicated more respect for her."

Doris was getting weaker by the day, rarely leaving her bedroom. She preferred that no one would see her in her weak state. Mother's Day was approaching and it was impossible for her daughter and son-in-law to be there. They arranged to have a present sent to her. The present was an "angel," a sensitive stylist named Tara Koenig. You see, her daughter had heard from her father, Doris's husband, that Doris needed a haircut. In her morning with shears, a smile and her natural sensitivity, she brought back Doris' will to live. Marlowe looked at his wife's new style and said, "You are beautiful." Renewed by her new look, she hoped for a party that weekend to see the family. All anyone talked about on Mother's Day was what Tara had done for their mom and grandmom. It was the best day Doris had in two years.

At Doris' eulogy a month later, the family was talking about how they would remember Mom. One of the memories was the look and the smile designed by Tara, the Rapid City hairdresser. Doris was my wife's mother and my mother-in-law.

And the angel, Tara, is every hairdresser in the world.

Thank you.

Dr. Lew

*When people ask what you do for a living,
simply respond,
"I cosmetically and psychologically
transform the self-images and destinies
of fellow human beings."*

- Dr. Lewis Losoncy

PSY-COSMETOLOGY

Technical Factors	+	People Factors	=	The New Professionalism
(Cosmetology)		(Psychology)		(Psy-Cosmetology)

Table of Contents

Thanks!

Thanks

There are a hundred thousand people responsible for the new profession of Psy-Cosmetology. The three who stand out for the credit for this book are our daughter Gabrielle Losoncy, and my friends Joe Santy, and Howard Hafetz.

Gabrielle researched, crafted, edited and expanded my thinking to give *On Becoming a Psy-Cosmetologist* a crisp, youthful feel. She knows every word in this book and understands every concept, and from my vantage point was my encourager because she believed in the importance of this work. She met every deadline and has fallen in love with hairdressers as much as they have fallen in love with her. Not bad for being just twenty-one!

Joe Santy, a Psy-Cosmetologist, a Pennsylvania salon owner and world reknowned guest artist kept this book practical and down to earth from his years of wisdom accumulated behind the chair, the desk and in his community. Joe and I had written a previous book together entitled Passionate Salon Professionals. His experiences as an educator in most of the US States, and a dozen foreign countries helped add an instructor's vantage point, as well to make the concepts more interesting and approachable. He left his chair to travel to Philadelphia for those now famous Wednesday meetings culminating with the inevitable celebration at The Black Sheep Pub. His love for his profession is heartwarming to experience.

And Howard Hafetz, where do I start? To begin to understand his impact, without Howard and his father, Joe Hafetz, I would never have been in any salon except to get my hair trimmed. Back in the 80's we saw a need and had a shared dream of a new profession of people, one who had the knowledge of both cosmetology and psychology, or expertise in understanding people. I was a practicing psychologist and a college professor who wrote books. And considering the lines of a popular song in those times, "To Sir, with Love," you could say Howard "had taken me from crayons to perfume." From writing books, to the beauty industry. Howard's numerous awards from the professional beauty industry would take pages to include. There are dozens and dozens of guest artists who Howard gave their first stage opportunity who today are seen on TV, and on the front covers of the major trade magazines. Howard is known in the Northeast for being CEO of the Raylon Corporation in Reading, Pennsylvania. He is also the publisher of this book. One whose ideas are present within these pages as well.

In addition, I thank the late Donald Scoleri, who was not only a great friend, a hairdresser, and talented salon business consultant but a previous co-author I had the privilege of knowing. And, of course thanks to my very special friends, Arnie and Sydell Miller with whom we shared a dream of changing the world together. And it happened! Dreams come true. Thanks for the most amazing ride of my life!

To my cuz (a Philadelphia term for a soul brother who is connected in the soul) Colin Walsh. We are on the same page. Colin and I wrote *On: A Brilliant Way to Live and Work.*

To Vicki Hafetz who when she believes in a dream is the best person I know who can ignite the fires under everyone to grab that dream. Thanks Vicki.

And to Diane, my wife, whose wisdom from the heart and eyes of both a hairdresser and a psychologist, was my constant guide.

In those hundreds of thousands of "Thank you," names, is yours as well.

Thanks to all of you.

Dr. Lew

Foreword by Howard Hafetz

This book is about your decision to create more passion, excitement, meaning, purpose, fulfillment, happiness and success in your life at work. To grow personally and professionally rather than to just get by, going to work, to make money to pay bills. Being a Psy-Cosmetologist ultimately means to be there in the salon not just to change hairstyles, but to change lives. This book is written for every person in the beauty profession, whether you are currently a student, instructor, stylist, manager, owner, or even guest artist.

It has been said that the teacher will arrive when the student is ready. This book is your teacher who will arrive and unfold for you at your readiness. Some of you will devour these ideas on your first day, dog-earring pages and calling for an immediate staff meeting. All you need is in your hands. In fact, reading just Part I in *On Becoming a Psy-Cosmetologist* will immediately change your view of your work. Part I alone is worth the investment of your time.

Most aware beauty schools will require their students to learn *On Becoming a Psy-Cosmetologist* to instill the motivation to continue their studies to earn their license in their important profession that changes peoples' lives. Students will learn seven healthy, motivating ways of looking at their lifework, as well as the six most important people skills for a stylist to be successful with clients. By the time you are through with half of this book, you will be wondering how you survived without these in your past.

Simply put, *On Becoming a Psy-Cosmetologist* is a keeper for life, a motivation book, a reference book, and a friend. Imagine having Dr. Lew with you 24/7!

I know you are going to enjoy every word and idea awaiting you in these pages.

Howard Hafetz

PSY-COSMETOLOGISTS:

Salon Professionals
Designing a More Beautiful-Feeling World

Imagine an electric map of just the United States and Canada with 160,000 bulbs illuminated across it. Let's call these lighted dots beauty salons and spas.

Within each of these salon bulbs, picture an average of four people. Then imagine that each of these four people see about forty clients a week. Actually, the word 'see' is an understatement – what they really do with those 26 million clients a week is 'touch', not just see. If we consider it more closely, however, even touch doesn't quite do justice to what is happening during these appointments. What is really going on is that these two thirds of a million people are influencing the appearances of the fellow human beings sitting in their hydraulic chairs.

And could it be that, in some cases, it goes even further than that? Could it be that some of those 26 million clients sitting in those chairs each week are actually feeling better about themselves and their lives? Could it be that in some cases, those clients are gaining a little more confidence, a little more courage, a little more hope during the time they spend with their stylist? Could it be that they are sharing things about their lives with this friend who touches them six to fifty times a year – more frequently than some of them see their friends and relatives?

What other profession in the world could make the claim of touching people on a regular basis for a period of years, consistently giving the life-changing gifts of beauty and confidence? Doesn't it give you a lift knowing that these 160,000 lighthouses are out there?

Did you ever see these facts before? Few people have!

I must be honest, before I took an in-depth look at the contributions of people in the professional salon industry, their impact simply went over my head. I started with the mission of helping the people working in those lighted dots to understand, from a psychologist's perspective, ways to serve their clientele more effectively. But as I ventured into the rich and unexplored terrain of the profession, I became overwhelmed with what I experienced. In fact, I almost turned back, convinced that no one would ever believe what was actually going on in these salons that you can find almost anywhere – from the crowded street corners of New York and Miami, to the winding country roads of West Virginia, to the golden wheat fields of Kansas, to the gallant snow-peaked Rockies of Alberta, Canada, to the Great Northwest and the lively streets of San Fransisco. When I am interviewed by news sources and radio stations, the story of my time with your – if I may be so bold, our – profession leads many reporters to be initially skeptical. As I elaborate, however, the interviewer's eyes brighten, recalling experiences that they or a loved one has had with stylists that they may have forgotten or not registered at the time. As I said in an interview with the Wall Street Journal when the reporter asked me if I was exaggerating things, "Before I spent time with open eyes to experience the power of the hairdresser, I would have agreed with you. If you spend the same amount of time, with the same open eyes, you will see what I am seeing."

In the initial manuscript, Donald Scoleri and I knew it was absolutely necessary to write about what we saw in salons every day. We needed to share with the world the fact that those two-thirds of a million people working in those 160,000 dots might be a source of strength for a large segment of society. And U.S. and Canada salons make up only 5% of the salons throughout the world! Our adventure revealed to us that what we were studying was possibly one of the most influential professions in the modern world. In these beacons of light are stationed a vast number of people who literally touch society at its very roots.

This book is about the journey through the profession of cosmetology, and how cosmetologists affect their clients. As you will soon see, it is a huge industry, a huge profession in dramatic transition. A major revolution is occurring in those lighthouses. The revolution is a human one; it is a transformation of self-image. The stylists are increasingly being seen for what they are – cosmetologists, who give the gift of beauty and confidence to their clients each day of the work week. These special professionals are increasingly taking on the challenge to be Psy-Cosmetologists, trained in communicating with people and understanding human behavior in addition to having the skills to enhance cosmetic beauty.

Have you noticed that neighborhood salons are turning into professional, quality service centers staffed with specialists in cutting, coloring, texturing, as well as skin, nail, and cosmetic care? The owners are gradually giving up their shears and turning to books to develop their expertise in business and people management.

I have tried to capture the new wave taking place in the professional salon industry. The ones who stand to gain the most from this Human Revolution are the 26 million clients who go to those 160,000 lighthouses each week. Perhaps the millions of salon professionals worldwide who make most of the public shine have been taken for granted.

For a few pages, I'd like to shine a little light on them!

7 BENEFITS OF BECOMING A PSY-COSMETOLOGIST

1. Finding more fulfillment in the salon, and in life

2. Increasing financial potential – LEARN MORE, EARN MORE

3. Achieving greater success with people

4. Acquiring skills to deal with all personalities

5. Learning strategies to cope with salon stresses

6. Experiencing more energy and motivation

7. Building your clientele and keeping your clientele

Part 1
THE HUMAN REVOLUTION OF PSY-COSMETOLOGY

Success in hairdressing, coloring, texturing, manicuring, pedicuring, waxing, massage or any service in the salon ultimately means success with people, doesn't it? Those are the people who choose to sit in your chair, experience your caring service, and feel the excitement of the new look you give them in the process.

That's where Psy-Cosmetology comes in. Psy-Cosmetology is the blending of the sciences of psychology and cosmetology. Psy-Cosmetologists use a holistic view – that is, they look at all factors to get a fuller understanding of a situation. They offer a **great look** on the **physical person** and **great feelings** in the **emotional person**. They know people don't want color in their hair just to have a new hair color. They want color in their hair to feel better about themselves.

The Psy-Cosmetologist has a greater awareness of her impact on the clients. That impact includes and transcends the person's physical features. The holistic Psy-Cosmetologist is aware of more than just a client's physical features. She considers many factors during a consultation:

- self-image, present and desired
- personality factors
- comfort change level
- lifestyle

Psy-Cosmetologists communicate caring through listening to learn about the unique, whole person in their chair.

As a salon professional, you spend thousands of hours studying the theory and practice of making people beautiful. Yet, we are increasingly realizing that your role requires both technical and emotional labor. Technical labor includes your styles, colors, professional recommendations, etc. Emotional labor involves your sensitivity and caring for the person sitting at your salon station. In fact, your profession involves as much emotional labor as any profession. This book has been written to complement your knowledge of hair, skin and nails with the knowledge and skills to be more effective with people, including your teammates, as well as your own understanding of how you can keep yourself enthused about your impact on people.

The Psy-Cosmetologist grows by studying psychology to gain a knowledge of human behavior, and to develop a sensitivity to help clients look and feel good through their human relations skills. These ideas will help provide you with the tools you need for the emotional labor of your lifework. You will discover how the science of psychology can help you develop your sensitivities and skills to be successful with people.

In Part I, you'll learn how Psy-Cosmetology began, and why salon professionals are so important in peoples' lives. You'll also experience the exhilaration of helping people of all ages and life experiences to look and feel better. And you will understand the differences between a Psy-Cosmetologist and a psychologist or a social worker, two professions that involve different education and expertise. The Psy-Cosmetologist is a salon professional who wants to build a more beautiful and confident world through their technical and human relations skills, one client at a time.

Chapter 1

Psy-Cosmetology:
The Beginnings of a New Profession

Definition (n.): *Psy-Cosmetology is the study of how a salon professional can cosmetically and psychologically transform self-images and destinies of fellow human beings.*

Psy-Cosmetology is the blending of the sciences of psychology and cosmetology. But why psychology? Because psychology is the study of human behavior. It's all about people, including understanding their personality, thoughts, feelings and what motivates their actions and their attitudes. Psychology can offer us ideas on how to be successful with all types of different personalities as well. And your success in the salon means success with people, doesn't it?

You might say Psy-Cosmetology is the study of how a salon professional can cosmetically and psychologically transform self-images and destinies of fellow human beings.

The Psy-Cosmetologist (1) has an inspiring view of life, (2) is self-motivated, (3) has great human relations skills, (4) values teamwork in the salon, (5) understands human behavior, and (6) is effective with all types of personalities. The first three of these will be covered in this book and the last three other points on teamwork, understanding human behavior, and dealing with all types of personalities will be addressed in other books.

Welcome to your journey of becoming a Psy-Cosmetologist. Allow me to introduce myself and the series of life-changing events I experienced that led me to write this book. Overnight I fell in love with your profession, and was determined to bring my interest in the psychology of encouraging people to cosmetologists everywhere. My name is Lew Losoncy. In the eighties, I was a therapist with a private practice in a downtown Reading, Pennsylvania office. At the same time, I was a professor of Psychology and chairman of the department of Behavior Science at the Reading Area Community College. One dramatic experience provided me the impetus to learn more about the beauty profession. Let me share with you the story of this event, which occurred during a therapy session with one of my patients, Debbie.

Debbie was an attractive 22-year-old woman whose major problem, shyness, kept her from reaching her goal of getting a date with a local accountant named David, She knew his patterns, the local lounges where he imbibed, and each Friday would go to a bar he frequented to try to get close to him. Each week David would ignore her and, frustrated, she would return to me to tell of her lack of progress with this "hunk."

After hearing the same thing week after week, I decided to encourage her to take a more assertive approach to fulfill her dreams of being with David.

"Maybe David himself is shy, Debbie. Perhaps he too would like to go out with you, but doesn't know how to go about it. I have a thought. Why don't you initiate a conversation with him, and if you two seem to click, you can ask him out to dinner."

"What? You mean me – just go up to him –" she shivered, " – and ask him out? A woman can't really do that, can she? I mean, wouldn't that be too pushy?"

"Well, Deb, apparently what you are doing now isn't working," I replied. "At worst, he'll ignore you, and that's exactly where you are right now, isn't it? Imagine if you and David would really hit it off. No limits!"

A thoughtful, anxious silence filled the room, and soon the young lady lifted her chin with determination and replied, "Okay, Dr. Lew, I'm going to talk to David on Friday. I'm going to go right up to him and ask him to go out to dinner. That's that."

She left the office determined to get that date.

My eagerness to hear the results of Debbie's plan made for a long week. When she arrived for her next appointment, her demeanor surprised me. Instead of Debbie prancing triumphantly into the room, in walked my client with a defeated, hang-dog expression. She slumped in her seat, and I initiated the conversation.

"Well, Deb, is there anything you'd like to tell me? I mean, did you talk to David on Friday?"

"Well, uh, no. I didn't," she timidly responded.

"Oh? Can you tell me why you didn't follow through on our plan?"

She responded with three sentences that changed my life! "Well, Doctor, I know you thought it would be a good idea to go talk to David. But, I talked to my hairdresser, and she thought it would be stupid. So I listened to her."

I was never the same again! Despite my ten years of schooling and both a Master's degree and Doctorate in helping people deal with life challenges, Debbie trusted her hairdresser's advice on a personal problem more than she did mine!

How could a hairdresser be so important in a person's personal life? How could doing a person's hair be so meaningful to a client? To answer that question, I decided to study the nature of that special relationship between hairdresser and client. But how could I get started?

A Psychologist Enters The Salon

Until this experience with Debbie, I hadn't thought often about hairdressers. Being unfamiliar with the beauty profession, and having a deep desire to learn about the stylist/client relationship, I had to search through my list of friends to get through the salon door.

Through a few contacts I was fortunate to meet the legendary Joe Hafetz, President of the Reading-based Raylon Distributorship. Joe had helped build thousands of salons by providing education and professional products to cosmetologists throughout the Northeast.

I was also privileged that day to meet his son Howard Hafetz, a far-thinking visionary who, at his young age, had already made dramatic contributions to the professional salon industry. We had much in common – both of us knew that there was much more to a haircut than just a haircut. We talked for hours, burning the midnight oil about what a hairstylist really does. He supplied the opportunity for me to work with thousands of salon owners, managers, stylists, receptionists, cleansing technicians, and other specialists. I had my "in." The remarkable journey to the center of the stylist/client relationship had begun.

Howard told me about a man on the West Coast who was more in touch with the very heart, mind, and soul of the hairstylist than anyone he knew. He explained that this man, Donald Scoleri, was at the time lecturing throughout North America, obsessed with upgrading the skills and images of salon industry professionals.

Howard conducted a program for stylists, owners and managers. Donald and I were the two lecturers. Although we met for the first time that day, it felt like the reunion of two old friends. Our ideas, mine from the field of psychology and Donald's from the field of cosmetology, were in tune. Psy-Cosmetology was born. Howard Hafetz had arranged what could eventually lead to changed perceptions of over half-a-million members of a profession who have started to see themselves as they really are – the most influential profession in society at the grass-roots level.

Donald made huge contributions to his profession including that initial book on Psy-Cosmetology until he passed away in 2011. This book builds on those insights and adds decades of wisdom that further reinforces the importance of salon professionals in today's world.

Why are hairdressers, barbers, specialists and the salon environments so important to the people whose lives they touch?

Summarizing the Major Points of Why Clients Trust Their Cosmetologist

As a psychologist, I wondered why my patient had such a deep trust in her stylist. The more I visited and studied salons, the more I began to understand why cosmetologists influence their clients' lives. I discovered three primary reasons for the special and unique relationship between the cosmetologist and the client:

• **Fact 1:** The cosmetologist is one of those rare professionals with a license to touch people.

• **Fact 2:** The cosmetologist sees the client on a regular, ongoing basis, and before most of the client's major life events.

• **Fact 3:** The cosmetologist has the power, the skills, and the tools to help the client look and feel more attractive and, in turn, more confident.

Let's explore each of these facts separately in the next three chapters.

Tips to Become a Psy-Cosmetologist

1. Appreciate the fact that while you work with hair, skin and nails, the true value of your work is on the people whose hair, skin and nails you are touching.

2. Understand the whole person whose life you are improving. What is her self-image, her personality, her change-comfort level and her lifestyle?

For any questions, further dialogue, or challenges with material in this chapter, please email us at howardh@peoplemediainc.com.

Chapter 2
Experience Your Power of Touch

One of the reasons for the cosmetologist's influence on people is because she is in one of those rare professionals with a license to touch people. The cosmetologist does what the lawyer, the teacher, the accountant, and the chairman of the board don't dare do. The cosmetologist touches people. In fact, there are only five professions who touch people; the doctor, the dentist, the nurse, the massage therapist and the cosmetologist. And for some of your clients, you are the only one who touches their lives. Your touch initiates the building of trust.

Touch is a vital need. The noted anthropologist Ashley Montagu wrote in his book, *Touching*, how we so frequently use words relating to the sense of touch to describe everyday experiences. Touch is so important that it influences much of our thinking, even in our language:

"We speak of rubbing people the wrong way . . . a soft touch . . . we get in touch or contact with others. Some people have to be handled carefully with kid gloves. Some are thick skinned, some get under one's skin, while others remain only skin deep . . . Some people are touchy."

Lack of Touch Hurts

Those who are touched tend to be healthier, warmer, and more emotionally stable people. Those who are not touched tend to be more aloof, cold, and suffering from emotional problems. In extreme cases, people die from lack of touch.

Two rival kings in the Middle Ages both believed his language to be the universal language and the language of the other king to be a fraud. They made a bet that, if young children were not talked to or touched, but just fed, the children would speak the true universal language, which each king believed to be his own language. They never found out which monarch was right, because all 24 infants died - not from lack of food, but from lack of touch.

The cosmetologist touches every client, every workday. The professional hair doctor is one of the few licensed professionals able to do so. But the hairdresser's power of touch goes even further than that. The cosmetologist may actually be healing diseases by fulfilling the client's important need for touch.

Touch May Be Healing

The scientific writer Charles Panati wrote in his book *Breakthroughs*:

"We realize that the human touch soothes, but it may also heal. In the future, doctors and nurses may be trained to hold their patients' hands or stroke their patients' injuries. In this way patients and children and spouses may to some extent become general physicians at home."

At the University of Maryland Medical School, Dr. James Lynch, a specialist in psychosomatic medicine, had found that petting animals has a beneficial effect on their cardiovascular systems; it also increases their resistance to infections. Similar results are being observed with human patients; even people in deep comas often register improved heart rate and brainwaves when their hands are held by doctors, nurses, or family members. Dr. Lynch extrapolates that these early findings for a broad human base. There is a biological basis for our need to form human relationships. He says, "If we fail to fulfill that need, our health is in peril."

Although those biological foundations have yet to be discovered, one new medical treatment called therapeutic touch is gradually being introduced into hospitals and nursing schools around the country. Simply stated, nurses attempt to make sick patients feel better by a sort of "laying on the hands." Pioneered by Dr. Dolores Krieger of New York University's School of Nursing, the therapy created a physical closeness between two people, even though the nurse never touches the patient but holds her hands about an inch above the patient's body (and not always the ailing part). Dr. Krieger suspects that the treating nurse actually transmits energy to the patient, which aids in recovery. Medical authorities are skeptical of that claim, but agree that, in many cases, therapeutic touch works. Stroking a fevered forehead, holding the hand of a suffering patient, or merely sitting because it raises the patient's spirits and, as a result, the bodily defenses. As holistic medicine teaches, anything that makes you feel better can also influence your recovery.

Touch may also be healing in another way. Massage therapists have begun teaching parents how to touch their babies with comfort and love. Tamsen Bruce, an Eastern Washington massage therapist, teaches parents how to touch and soothingly stroke their newborns. Some champions of infant massage say that not only is it soothing for the child, but becoming aware of feeling in the baby's body could very well prevent child abuse. What a gift to give a parent... and a baby, and a relaxed future salon client.

So far thousands of doctors, nurses, therapists, and even some veterinarians have mastered the technique of therapeutic touch, and their number is steadily growing. More hospitals are permitting their staffs to practice the treatment as an adjunct to - never in place of - conventional therapies. Only future experiments will determine whether touching heals for physical or psychological reasons. In the meantime, we may see physicians in the next decade of the 2000s prescribing less medication and dispensing a lot more Tender Loving Care.

Think of it: the cosmetologist is licensed to touch each client, every workday. And it is true that in some cases the hairstylist may be the only one who touches a client in his or her adult life. This is especially reassuring, because in today's technological society, people's need for touch is being fulfilled even less.

The More Technology in Our World, The More We Need Touch: The Beauty Profession is the Place to Be in Today's World

In his bestselling book *Megatrends*, John Naisbitt advanced the argument that the more technology that exists in our world, the more people have a need for personal touch (literal and figurative). Perhaps, in a way, the world is becoming less personal with our dependence on the Internet. People tend to feel more like "things" or "numbers" or "its" instead of people. Most of us are identified with a social security number, a license plate number, an insurance policy number, a credit card number, a telephone number, an IP address number and a postal number.

Since Naisbitt's book first appeared the proliferation of technology has expanded exponentially and today there is an even greater craving for healthy human contacts.

From our vantage point, there is no place in communities of today and of the future that is in a better position to fulfill people's need for touch than in the salon, with the warm touch of a stylist who knows our name. A stylist's everyday way of touching people, rarely realized, is a great factor in the special relationship with clients, and its importance goes beyond just a haircut. It fulfills one of the most basic human needs, the need for touch. The Psy-Cosmetologist's primary point of difference is a deep sensitivity to the touching contact she has with her client, starting with the shampooing.

Shampooing is A Touching Experience

The shampooing done by a relaxed person who makes minimal demands on clients to think, talk, or answer questions can be anything from a relaxing to a sensual experience. Clients trust the cleansing technician enough to touch their hair, even if it's dirty or ill-kept. And the cleansing technician accepts these clients without reprimand. Even their parents didn't do that! And so, the trust begins to build. A deep unspoken communication is taking place in that soothing, relaxing, cleansing, massaging experience between the professional hands of the Psy-Cosmetologist and the client's scalp and shoulders. Psy-Cosmetologists consciously put into their professional hands a message of, "I care. You are special." And "I want to be here. I want to help." Or even "I love working with your hair," like, "I am enjoying this as much as you are."

The Psy-Cosmetologist Offers Unconditional Acceptance

Psychologists learn how to create a special relationship, a bond, between themselves and their patients that has the quality of "unconditional acceptance." Unconditional acceptance is the feeling that exists in the best, most wholesome relationships. Unconditional acceptance is a way of behaving that communicates to the other, "I accept you with no conditions, no strings attached. You can feel safe to express yourself without any pressure or fear of judgment. I have positive feelings for you based upon you being you, even if your hair is not perfect." Couple unconditional acceptance with the relaxing experience of having one's hair washed and you begin to see the depth of the relationship that occurs in the shampooing setting.

In that touching setting, something else is occurring. Cosmetologists are washing away their clients' masks, their psychological defenses. My friend, the famous artist Charles Henry Norman, says that in a three hour sitting with famous figures, giving them his sole attention while sketching in their facial details, they tell him more about themselves than they have told some long-time friends. Norman explains, "you are addressing flaws about themselves head on that they are anxious about. And you still accept them. The contact is close." Charles is noted for his sketch of President Dwight Eisenhower – his work is the way the world will remember "Ike."

The cleansing technician, like the artist, is in charge, is benign, is accepting without conditions, and is interested. The client's fears, anxieties, and resistances are lowered. The client feels safe, even in an unprotected state. A shampoo would be the logical start of a therapeutic salon experience even if shampoos weren't necessary. It is the forerunner to the blossoming of beauty that occurs soon after.

Styling is Touching To Remove the Less Desirable Parts

The stylist wields scissors, an aggressive weapon. From childhood, people have been cautioned to be careful when using knives and scissors. Yet clients trust that the cosmetologist will use this power tool to help them, not hurt them. They trust that the stylist will be discriminating enough to remove only the undesirable hairs! They eagerly lift their heads at the stylist's will. For a period of time in their visit to the salon, they trust the stylist to see them at their worst, and he or she still accepts them.

The relationship in some cases is so strong that many clients demand the individual attention of their stylists. Their annoyance while waiting in the reception area is many times related to the stylist's being with another client. Leaving a client to accept a personal phone call is sometimes perceived as a rejection, or at least a statement that "something else is more important than me." Stylists have described clients who would ask them, "About how many people will you see today?" The question could certainly be a reflection of the feeling, "Am I just another customer to you?" Maybe even, "How many people do I share you with?" Perhaps, "Am I special?"

And, finally, always keep in mind that, for a few of the clients in those chairs of change, the Psy-Cosmetologist may be the only one who touches him or her in their life!

Along with the cosmetologist's license and ability to satisfy clients' needs for touch, the second reason for the powerful relationship is the frequency of contact.

Summarizing the Major Points of Why the Power of Touch Is Important

- **Fact 1:** The cosmetologist is one of only five professions with a license to touch people, and touch builds trust.

- **Fact 2:** Touch may not only build trust; it may be healing.

- **Fact 3:** In shampooing, touch creates a cleansing experience.

- **Fact 4:** Touching people reveals a stylist's unconditional acceptance of the client.

Touching Tips

1. Be fully aware when you are touching your client. During the shampooing, make sure that the water temperature is perfect and be conscious of how your hands feel on her scalp.

2. Experience your shampooing as cleansing her and helping her to feel cleaner and more beautiful.

If you've found these ideas meaningful, consider reading the book *Touching: The Human Significance of the Skin* by Ashley Montagu.

For any questions, further dialogue, or challenges with material in this chapter, please email us at howardh@peoplemediainc.com.

Chapter 3
Affect a Lifetime of Important Moments

The cosmetologist sees the client on a regular, ongoing basis, and before every major life event. Delving into the nature of the relationship between hairdresser and client is, to say the least, an eye-opening experience. Yes, you find that hairdressers touch people, but the relationship goes much further than that. Hairdressers see each client six to fifty times a year, sometimes over a period of twenty years or longer. How many times a year do most of these clients see their relatives?

A survey done several years back by Modern Salon Magazine revealed that one out of four clients had been going to the same cosmetologist for longer than seven years. Interestingly, male clients had even more stylist loyalty than female clients.

Unlike the schoolteacher who is with a child for a period of only one year (on rare occasions, two years), and unlike the doctor who often sees a patient only once or twice a year for a checkup, the professional hair stylist is a regular in the client's life, sometimes even considered "family." The lawyer is called in only in times of crisis. Dentists see patients every six months, barring an emergency. Only the relationship with one's religious advisor is more frequent, but even that is not always on a personal, one-on-one, touching basis.

The power of the Psy-Cosmetologist/client relationship goes beyond mere frequency. The cosmetologist is around people during family births, family deaths, and all touchstone events in between.

A Haircut Is A Good Reason To Bring People Together Again

The public perception of what cosmetologists do is that "they cut hair." If a stylist just cuts hair, why do the hair professionals we meet know most of their clients' husbands', wives', girlfriends', and boyfriends' names? In some cases, they know both the client's wife and the client's girlfriend! And in some communities, they cut the husband's, the wife's, and the girlfriend's hair! As we said before, it is a touchy business!

If hairstylists just cut hair, why do they know about their clients' children's school problems? Why do they know about their clients' talents, trophies, and achievements? If hairstylists just cut hair, why do they get cookies, lasagna, and even liquor from their clients? Does a doctor? Does a dentist? Do you take homemade bread to your accountant? Do you stop in to say hello if you are in your lawyer's neighborhood? Probably not.

The Psy-Cosmetologist/client relationship is unique. That uniqueness became clear to me while observing a kindergarten teacher discussing "community helpers" with her six year olds.

"What do we call the person who helps you when you are sick?"

"A doctor!"

"Very good Olivia."

"What do you call the person who cleans and fixes your teeth?"

"That's a dentist!"

"Right again Olivia."

"What do you call the person who puts the fire out in a building?"

"That's a fireman!"

"That's right Seth."

"Very good class. Doctor, dentist, fireman."

"And what do you call the person who does your hair and makes you pretty?"

"Oh, that's Ginger!"

Could be any doctor, dentist or fireman in a generic category. But not the little girl's hairdresser. That's Ginger!

Two people are united over a cosmetic service appointment six to fifty times a year. In this process, touching, sharing, and communication between two human beings takes place. They go through the years of life together.

Psy-Cosmetologists Encourage Personal Growth of Both Inner and Outer Self-Image

Otto Rank, the noted psychiatrist, saw life as a constant series of choices. One choice is to grow, to move forward and to seek newness. The alternative is to retreat, to stagnate, and to cling to the past with its sameness and its predictability. We are constantly faced with the decision to make growth or stagnation decisions in our lives.

> *Growth decisions occur when we make the decision to go out of our comfort zone in order to improve ourselves.*

Whether we are willing to risk growth or not is at least partially related to the significant, constant others in our lives. When we are in the presence of discouraging people, we are more likely to make stagnation decisions. And with close encouragement, support and warmth from significant others, we are more likely to make courageous, growth decisions. Growth decisions occur when we make the decision to go out of our comfort zone in order to improve ourselves.

Growth versus stagnation points are especially heightened during major changes in our lives. One such crucial time is the first day of kindergarten. Some children run eagerly into the new social setting, mingle with others, and adapt to life's next step (growth decision). Other children cling to mommy or daddy with tear-filled eyes, and need to be pulled like chewing gum from their parent's legs (stagnation decision). A Psy-Cosmetologist's encouragement helps the client to make growth decisions; and, by making growth decisions, we experience our inner self-image growing as well.

A Psy-Cosmetologist Encourages the Person Under The Hair

I mention this example of kindergarten because of a touching experience I witnessed years ago between Jonathan, a five-year-old tyke, and his stylist of three years, Jean. I've tried to capture their dialogue.

Jonathan: You know what Jean? I start kindergarten tomorrow.

Jean: I know, Jonathan, and we're going to make you the most handsome boy there!

Jonathan: Can you make me look like Ron Kittle? (a then-Chicago baseball player)

Jean: Old Jean is going to make you look like a real baseball player. Are you excited about school, Jonathan?

Jonathan: I'm scared, a little. Mom says if you don't listen, the teacher gets mad and yells.

Jean: Sometimes doing new things is scary. But, honey, remember the first time you slept at your Aunt Paula's house and were scared of being away from home?

Jonathan: With Mickey and Tommy?

Jean: Yes. You were scared, but you wound up having fun, didn't you?

Jonathan: Yeah! We played baseball and stayed up real late!

Jean: Yes. See, I think kindergarten's going to be fun. And I wouldn't worry about the teacher getting mad and yelling. I'll just bet the teacher is going to love you. You know how much I love you, don't you?

Jonathan: (giggles, puts hands over his little mouth)

Jean: Okay, my little first baseman, go get them in school tomorrow, and see you in a couple.

Jonathan: See you in a couple, Jean. I'm gonna tell my teacher about you tomorrow. Bye.

How much would that Psy-Cosmetologist be worth to you if you had a son with kindergarten anxiety? How important was the actual haircut?

Psy-Cosmetologist Jean before Jonathan's First Day of School

Jean will probably see Jonathan before he graduates from elementary school, before his first junior high baseball game, before his first date, before he gets his high school class picture taken, before his graduation, and standing in the receiving line at Jonathan's wedding, telling his bride how cute Jonathan was the first day before he started kindergarten. And, do you know that his bride will be very interested in this information about her husband's early days, from a person who was there, the Psy-Cosmetologist?

Following the therapeutic dialogue, I asked Jean if I could borrow a blow-dryer to fan the tears dry. I told her how touching it was for me to see how she helped a little tyke to go forward and eagerly face a tough new life experience.

Apologetically, she replied, "Oh, I don't deserve that, I'm only a hairdresser!"

Do you think that Jean is only a hairdresser? In our new age of awareness, we don't hear, "I'm just a hairdresser," anymore. We hear a proud assertion – "I'm a hairdresser!"

Psy-Cosmetologist Carol and Client Helen: Planning for the Final Makeover

Carol had been Helen's stylist for twenty-seven years of Wednesday mornings in her Naperville, Illinois salon. In twenty-seven years you can get to know a person quite well. Helen was getting increasingly more ill and one Tuesday she called Carol and said she couldn't make it into the salon for her standing appointment. She asked Carol if she could visit her at home before opening up the salon in the morning.

Of course Carol agreed.

It was there that Helen revealed, "You know Carol. I'm very ill. I just ask one thing from you. You know I'm a control freak and don't trust anybody to make decisions for me. But if something happens to me, could you please be there and have me looking my best?"

"Helen, we'll have another twenty-seven years of Wednesdays together. But just in case I want to reassure you that you will be looking perfect."

Helen breathed a sigh of relief.

Less than ten hours later Ben, Helen's husband called Carol with the sad news of her death. He then thanked Carol for being there for Helen every Wednesday.

Helen looked perfect a few days later.

And the minister reassured the congregation, "She had Carol her hairdresser with her along with Ben throughout her adult life. What a difference one hairdresser can make in a person's life."

Summarizing the Major Points of Affecting a Lifetime of Important Moments

- **Fact 1:** Cosmetologists are with their clients before every important lifetime experience.
- **Fact 2:** The Psy-Cosmetologist views the salon experience as a reason to get closer to their clients.

Tips to Go through the Years with Your Client

1. Experience your client as having a life outside of the salon – a life you will be influencing her to feel more courageous and confident in living.

2. Be sensitive to your relationship with your client, because you are going through the years with her. Talk about memories and looks she had in the past and discuss new looks she might choose for her future.

3. Be aware of important events in her life. Talk about them and share your awareness of them with her.

For any questions, further dialogue, or challenges with material in this chapter, please email us at howardh@peoplemediainc.com.

Chapter 4
Psy-Cosmetologists Help People Both Look and Feel Good

The cosmetologist has the professional skills and the tools to help the client look and feel more attractive, and, in turn, more confident. In addition to touch and frequency of contact, a third uniqueness about the Psy-Cosmetologist/ client relationship is that the helper has the professional powers and abilities to impart beauty, which could also mean greater confidence.

A doctor tends to the medical health of a patient. A cosmetologist can't. A dentist tends to the dental health of a patient. A cosmetologist can't. An accountant tends to the fiscal health of a client. A cosmetologist can't. A lawyer tends to the legal health of a client. A cosmetologist can't. The Psy-Cosmetologist or the P.H.D. – Professional Hair Stylist – tends to the hair, skin, and nail health of a client, which the doctor, dentist, accountant, lawyer, teacher, electrician, plumber, librarian, and chairman of the board can't. Beauty is the cosmetologist's area of expertise, his or her "niche."

A clean bill of health from a doctor can give you confidence about one's physical well being. A cavity-free checkup can give one confidence for six months about one's teeth and gums. Balanced, accurate books can give one confidence against an IRS audit. A roofer's skills can reassure one that the squirrels won't be living with the family. Victory in a court case can give one confidence about staying out of jail.

Keep in mind that the Psy-Cosmetologist gives confidence in self, the very core of the personality. And when you have self-confidence, you can get almost anything you want!

Salon Professionals are Artists of People

The master diamond cutter works only on a thing, a stone, albeit a valuable one. A cosmetologist designs a breathing, alive human being who shines as a result of the treatment. The client can change and can feel much more than the shiny stone.

The greatest artists in the world, the Van Goghs, the Monets, the Picassos, did their work on a mere canvas. The cosmetologist's canvas is a person. The canvas of an artist does not ask to look a certain way. The canvas is discarded if too many errors are made. The salon artist works not on mere canvas, but on a fellow human being, who in some cases asks to look a certain way and certainly cannot be discarded, but lives on as a continual reminder of the artist's work.

Research on the Importance of Beauty in Our Lives

The most thorough book on the topic of the influence of beauty on behavior I've found is *The Psychology of Cosmetic Treatments* by Jean Ann Graham and Albert M. Kligman. In citing a study with teachers by Margaret Clifford and Elaine Hatfield the researchers concluded that children who look better were judged to be more intelligent, more interested in furthering their education, and were viewed as having parents who were more interested in their schooling. Teachers also expected good looking students to be more popular as well as brainy, and assumed they would get along well with their classmates. Keep in mind the teachers never met the students, but just saw pictures of them. They included the same resumes but just changed the picture of the student.

Numerous others studies revealed that personnel managers and employers are more likely to hire good looking men and women, to pay them more, and to promote them more readily.

One of the first things a criminal attorney does is to have the client get his or her grooming act together. Why? Judges and juries are more lenient on good looking defendants. Plus good looking people are less likely to get caught in illicit activities. And if caught, they are less likely to be reported.

Psy-Cosmetologists, as well as all ethical people, do not believe that it is right to judge any student, employee, patient of defendant on appearance, but rather on true character. However, facts are facts. And a nice, new look is not illegal.

The Psy-Cosmetologist's Mission: To Help People Feel, Look and Be Beautiful

Can you tell us a greater mission than helping people be their best?

Watch people when they come into a salon. Watch them when they leave. The difference, whether measured in facial expression, height of chin or proud shoulders, was a professional hairstylist who gave time, attention, touch, caring, and a hairstyle. How important is that contact to the client's confidence?

- How many people stay home instead of going out for the evening because they feel that they don't look their best? Yet, the following night, after they visit their hairdresser, they will go out.

- Stylists can tell when one of their clients met someone new on the social scene by the "can you fit me in today, as soon as possible?" syndrome.

- Before the president of the United States goes on TV to make a firm, persuasive statement to the world, who do you think will be one of the last people to see him before his talk?

- Many stylists say that the elderly person who goes shopping once a week does so only on the day of his or her visit to the salon.

- One salon owner and stylist combs and works on the hair of a major Midwestern city mayor every morning before his day at city hall. The mayor's chauffeur told me that this is an important part of his day, to give him the lift he needs to lead his people and to learn what the people in his city are thinking out there in the real world.

- Lew M., a hairstylist from Minneapolis, Minnesota, is the only reason why a psychotically depressed patient could get out of the mental hospital every five weeks. Lew know how to cut to avoid painful reminders of disease and treatment. He was told that the patient remained free from depression for several days after she returned from her haircut appointment.

We could go on and share another thousand stories to support the cosmetologist's power to help people feel and be beautiful, and how feeling beautiful gives confidence. So could you, if you just stop to think about it.

A Springfield, Illinois barber friend, Bernie Koch, observed, "People don't come to us for a haircut. They come to us for courage, confidence, and hope."

Let us simply ask you this: If Susie Harris is going to be at the altar in white early tomorrow, where will she be today? With the doctor? With the engineer? With the chairman of the board? NO! She'll be with the second most important person in her life for a period of time – her hairstylist.

The Psy-Cosmetologist touches people, removes their masks and defenses, is with them on a regular, ongoing basis during crucial life periods, and has the tools to make people be and feel beautiful, thus confident. Whew!!

Summary of the Major Points of Helping People Look and Feel Good

- **Fact 1**: Psy-Cosmetologists are artists – not on things, but on people.
- **Fact 2:** Psy-Cosmetologists believe that people want to look good for the purpose of feeling good about themselves.
- **Fact 3:** Research reveals that helping people look good gives them physical, emotional, psychological, social, and inspirational advantages.

Tips to Help People Look and Feel Good

1. Open your client's eyes to the fact that their new look doesn't just make them better physically, but helps them become better socially, emotionally, psychologically, physically, and maybe even spiritually.

2. Realize that people don't just want color in their hair to have new color in their hair – rather, they want to feel more color and excitement in their life.

If you've found these ideas to be meaningful, consider reading the book *The Psychology of Cosmetic Treatments* by Jean Ann Graham.

For any questions, further dialogue, or challenges with material in this chapter, please email us at howardh@peoplemediainc.com.

Part 2
PSY-COSMETOLOGISTS ARE SELF-MOTIVATED
The Psy-Cosmetologists' 7 Sources of Personal Motivation

Love Life
Be Driven from Within
Change People's Lives
Be Open to Grow
Highlight Your Strengths
Get over Stuff
Quickly Find a Way

Psy-Cosmetologists Are Self-Actualizing

Your new field of psychology experienced a dramatic transformation decades ago. This change involved shifting the focus from what was wrong with people, to looking for what was right with people. Disease-centered psychology was giving way to looking for a person's strengths and potential. A great deal of the credit for that change was due to the optimist psychologist, Abraham Maslow. Maslow was determined to understand the qualities of the happiest and most fulfilled people. He called them "self-actualizing humans," because they were actualizing or bringing out more of their fuller potential.

> *"self-actualizing humans," because they were actualizing or bringing out more of their fuller potential.*

Curiously, the common patterns Psy-Cosmetologists have are very similar to those self- actualizing individuals. As you discover the most fulfilling ways of living, you will experience yourself growing and, you could say, self-actualizing. How do self-actualizing people move through life?

Qualities of The Self-Actualizing Person

1. The self-actualizing person is more **spontaneous**. They trust their guts! In many ways they are childlike and choose to get into each moment more fully. They see more, feel more, taste more, hear more and touch more of life (Chapter 5 discusses how a self-actualizing person's spontaneity is similar to the Psy-Cosmetologist's **love of life**). The self-actualizing stylist is one who spontaneously envisions a brand new look on a client.

What is something that really excites you and makes you feel creative?

_____

_____

2. The self-actualizing person is a self-starter who is **independent of culture and environment for motivation**. Self-actualizers are self-motivated and don't need to be pushed, praised or punished from the outside world. Even if everything is going wrong and everyone else is bummed out, self-actualizers use their attitude tools to keep themselves going. (The Psy-Cosmetologist is **driven from within** and is determined to rise above any challenge, as you'll experience in Chapter 6). The self-actualizing salon professional is motivated for each day with goals and plans.

In what part of your life would you like to become more motivated?

_____

_____

3. The self-actualizing person has **deeper and more meaningful relationships**. Also the self- actualizing person **discriminates between means and ends**; that is, **sees each moment as an end in itself**, not just as a means to another end later. They don't go to work today because of the pay they will receive in two Fridays. Their rewards aren't limited to once every fourteen days, but rather everyday. They are in the salon today for the rewarding purpose of making people beautiful.

In other words, combining these two characteristics, the self-actualizing salon professional doesn't view people as means to an end things to be used, but people are viewed as an end in themselves. (Similarly, the Psy-Cosmetologist **changes peoples' lives** in the salon.

The client, or the person in the chair, is not an "it," or an "11 o'clock," but is "Susan," whose life the Psy-Cosmetologist is determined to improve as you'll read in Chapter 7).

Who is a person whose life you have helped change? How?

_____

_____

4. The self-actualizing salon professional is **growth-centered, not self-centered**. Self-centered people are closed to new ideas and are totally wrapped up in trying to avoid making mistakes, clinging to their own old habits, handcuffed by the fear of failure. Self-actualizing stylists are growth-centered and are open to learn, grow and even value criticism, thanking their critics if their ideas help them to grow. (In Chapter 8, you'll experience how the Psy-Cosmetologist is **open to grow** from all sources, including their instructor's, salon manager's or clients' suggestions on how they might become even better.)

What is something you would like to learn about or learn how to do?

_____

_____

5. The self-actualizing salon professional has a **continued freshness of appreciation**. Self- actualizing persons have the wonderful capacity to appreciate freshly again and again the basic good things of life with wonder and even ecstasy – however stale, routine, and unnoticed these experiences might be to others. "Thus for a self-actualizing person any sunset may be as beautiful as the first one, any flower may be of breath-taking loveliness, even after she has seen a million flowers" Maslow observed. (The Psy-Cosmetologist **moves from positives** and is inspired by what is right in oneself, others, in life, and in the salon as you'll discover in Chapter 9.)

What is the best quality you have? How do you use it?

_____

_____

6. The self-actualizing salon manager has a **more accepting perception of reality**. The healthiest and happiest people are secure and do not have to twist facts to fit their own emotional needs, or their personal, "shoulds." They don't have to lie to themselves that reality need be any different than the way it is. When it rains, they don't waste time complaining, they simply grab an umbrella. When they are in an accident they simply get the information necessary and take their car to be repaired. That's it. (The Psy-Cosmetologist is realistic, **gets over stuff,** and quickly accepts reality, as you'll find in Chapter 10).

Name a setback in your life that you overcame. What helped you "get over it?"

_____

_____

7. The self-actualizing stylist is **creative**. Because they are not afraid of making mistakes, they are able to bring out the best in themselves. They have an underlying belief that through their unlimited creative minds, there is an answer to every challenge. They look up, rather than down, when facing a tough situation, and their belief in themselves gives them the motivation to go forward. (The Psy-Cosmetologist creatively **finds a way**, overcoming the challenges on the road to success. You will be finding ways as you read Chapter 11).

What is a challenge you solved with creativity?

_____

_____

_____

_____

_____

As you compare Maslow's list to the qualities of a Psy-Cosmetologist, you will find that from a psychological perspective, these special salon professionals are self-actualizers. Here in Part II, these next 7 chapters focus on developing better self-awareness and building our inner drive to get more out of each day, perhaps even each moment. In the process of becoming a Psy-Cosmetologist, we will experience the fringe benefit of self-actualizing.

Chapter 5
Love Life

You are alive! Being alive gives you opportunities and hope. You are alive to create your day. Will you make today a repeat of yesterday, or will you fill today with new experiences and creations? Are you going to live fully today, or to use up today by re-living yesterday?

After three decades of having the honor of working with salon professionals, it became obvious to me that there were personality similarities woven throughout the happiest, healthiest, most productive stylists, colorists, perm specialists, nail technicians, skin care specialists and massage therapists. Whether I visit Portland, Oregon or Portland, Maine, Rio de Janeiro, Brazil, or Zagreb, Croatia, I experience enthusiastic stylists of all ages, usually seated right up front in class, with a notepad or a computer, ready to learn and grow. They arrive at the program early, are enthusiastic about the day and are filled with an *overall love of life.*

Psy-Cosmetologists also have a great sense of humor. My friends in Wyoming had me believing in the existence of animals called "jackelopes." I chased a "snipe" in Kansas, and was concerned about "flying, attacking koala tree bears" jumping from the trees in Melbourne, Australia. They are up for adventure and fun! These special salon professionals say "yes!" to life, and enjoy the freshness of each day, each moment.

"Nothing is fresher than this moment, Dr. Lew," a Denver Psy-Cosmetologist told me. She added, "You don't have to get out of a rut if you never let yourself get into one in the first place." The earth moved when she laughed. Like a constantly uncorking bottle of champagne, the woman, appropriately named Surprise, brought an appreciation of life to everyone fortunate enough to be in her presence.

What are some ways to develop an even greater love of life?

1. Realize "You Are Alive!"

2. Know That the "Now Moments" Are the Real Gems of Life

3. Be MINDFUL (Aware of Your Experiences)

4. Put Yourself into a State of FLOW (Finding Deeper Meaning in Your Work)

5. Take Time to Appreciate What You Already Have

1. Realize "You Are Alive!"

Pause for a moment and realize your aliveness. This is your own unique moment in the long history of the universe. This is your time to shine. And you yourself are nothing short of a once in a lifetime miracle. You are such a rare combination of the physical and spiritual that there is no one, anywhere in the world exactly like you. You are so special that you have been given the greatest gift in the world. You were selected to be a human. You are the owner of your body, your mind, your actions, your thoughts and your feelings. Even your dreams are uniquely yours. You are also the director of environmental engineering to build the world you live in. And this is your day to make and shape. You are alive today, which gives you the power to draw up the blueprint for the kind of person you are in the process of becoming.

To increase the awareness of your aliveness, shout to your body and mind the words, "I am alive!" Let your heart hear those powerful words. You are alive... and that wouldn't have to be. Don't take a moment of today for granted, because it will soon pass into irretrievable yesterdays.

In your awareness of your aliveness, and your awareness of the power you have over this impermanent day, create a sense of urgency for this moment. Now pause again and tell yourself this fact: "Today is the most important day of my life, because it is the only day I can change now!" Say it again: "Today is the most important day of my life, because it is the only day I can change now!" Yesterday is recorded, tomorrow is unreachable, but today is in front of you.

Each Moment is Fresh and New

Think of it: The universe is giving you this moment fresh, new, open, shape-able to your will. What will you write on this blank slate of today? Will you write with all of the colors of the rainbow a whole new, exciting story on your blank slate of today, or will you rewrite the same old story of yesterday? Will you live this precious moment as the first as it truly is, or use up this important, unique day by robotically re-living a previous day. That's not living, that's re-living. Think of yourself as an architect of your future in this moment, not as an archaeologist digging up your past.

Or will you use up today consumed with all of the worries, drained by the "what-ifs" of the future. That's not living, that's pre-living. How many things have you worried about in your past, creating hours of pain over events that never even occurred? Or if it did occur, you're still here, aren't you? You can't cross the bridge until you get to it anyway, can you?

Forget re-living. Stop pre-living. And start living. Grab hold of your real power. You are alive. You have today. You have now! What more could you possibly need?

2. Know That the "Now Moments" are the Real Gems of Life

- What is the most important job in your life? The one you are doing now!

- Who is the most important person in your life? The person you are with now!

- What is the most important day in your life? The one you are living now!

You have about two and one half billion **now moments** of life (treating each now moment as a second). Each now moment is new, and unique. The quality of our life is dependent on our awareness that we can create new thoughts, feelings, actions and dreams in any one of these now moments. It is in our now moments that we find our opportunities to learn, grow, create and succeed. These moments don't occur just on pay day. Every day can be a pay day. How many firsts can you have today? Or more accurately, how many firsts will you make happen today?

Don't just saunter through life today. Step through your day with a brisk pace. Own your life. Make things happen. When you get high on life, you can change the world. Imagine what you could accomplish in just one day of your life with your enthusiasm power! Consider this:

In one day, you could have breakfast in New York City, lunch in Vancouver, British Columbia, and settle down for a roast pig dinner in Honolulu.

In one day, you could travel one-seventh of the way to the moon. But if you don't have a full two weeks to spend traveling to and from the moon, just wait. In the oncoming years, it will take even less of your valuable "alive" time.

In one day, you could produce the beginnings of a new life. In one day, you could put a smile on hundreds of faces.

In one day, Mother Theresa, the Nobel Peace Prize winner, fed tens of thousands of children in India.

In one day – in fact, in just 12-15 seconds – the pit crew at an Indianapolis 500 race can change all of the tires on a car.

Ignite your enthusiasm – the power system to success. Think of the possibilities you have in just one day when you are enthusiastic. What could you possibly do with your unlimited talents, unlimited assets, unlimited creative ideas and unlimited enthusiasm in only one day? Well, brace yourself; not only do you have one of these days available to you, you probably have 30,000 or more of these days available in your lifetime.

Bring out your enthusiasm for the day. Psychologists tell us that we can change our life by either changing our thoughts or changing our behavior. By acting as if we are enthused, our feelings and thoughts will change as a result. So how do you become enthusiastic? By becoming enthusiastic!

1. Wake up enthusiastically. In the morning, when most people treat their alarm clocks like the enemy, look at your alarm clock as though it were a friendly fire

alarm. When it rings, jump out of bed fired up with your enthusiasm. Put a glow in your mind and heart. An enthusiastic start to the day gives you an advantage over the ho-hum person who needs a morning cup of coffee or a smoke to get going. Let your fire alarm ignite action and enthusiasm for the day. Remember, the way to become enthusiastic is to become enthusiastic.

2. Smile enthusiastically. Wherever you go, watch the life-giving power that your smile has on people. We have asked thousands of people the question, "Who would you rather be with, an enthusiastic person or a person with a frown?" Does it surprise you to discover that not one single person preferred a frowning person? Be the energy wherever you go. Even if at first it seems unnatural to extend a warm welcoming smile to everyone, it will soon be as natural to you as tying your shoes.

To realize the power of a smile, let's consider two people. We'll call the first person, who never smiles, I.M. Dull. How do you feel around I.M. Dull? I.M. Dull isn't very rewarding to be around. Would you buy anything from I.M. Dull? Would you enjoy listening to a lecture given by I.M. Dull? Probably not. Now consider the other person, a good listener, who meets you with a warm smile. This person is very successful at promoting professional services and products, isn't she? Let's call this person N. Thusiastic. Isn't N. Thusiastic a more refreshing person to be around? Doesn't this person give you more life than I.M. Dull?

Get enthused about yourself. Become determined that you will light up the faces of people with your smile; then watch your energy level climb like a spaceship ascending from the launching pad at Cape Kennedy.

3. Walk enthusiastically. Enthusiasts walk faster. They should – they are going places. Compare the walks of I.M. Dull and N. Thusiastic. While I.M. Dull walks with head down, shoulders curved inward, and a short apologetic step, N. Thusiastic walks with head up (even in the rain), shoulders back, and a crisp gait. Without meeting these two individuals, you draw conclusions about them just by observing their walks. Their walks tell a story.

4. Speak enthusiastically. Modulate your voice. Every person can remember a never- ending speech given by a monotonous speaker. Yet the same words, brought to life by an enthusiastic speaker, can give energy to the group and make the talk more powerful. You can probably also remember teachers who gave no excitement to their lessons. Or perhaps you experienced a salesperson who just described a house, a car, or a living room set, with no life or panache. Listen to two stylists describing the same shampoo to a client. The one using more upbeat words is more exciting and more successful. The enthusiast puts vitality into their message.

Hold people's attention by putting refreshment into everything you say. Say "hello" with life. Say "congratulations" with vigor. Say "have a great day" with meaning and genuine enthusiasm. When you "vitalize" things, something interesting happens. You actually invigorate yourself. When someone asks you how you are doing, do you just say "okay" or "not so good"? Enliven your response and watch how you can change your "okay" or "not so good" to "terrific!" or "fantastic!" You actually do become terrific or fantastic just by saying and feeling it.

5. Answer your cell phone enthusiastically. Get off automatic pilot and get enthused every time the phone rings. Remember, the person calling is someone who is taking the time to phone you. You are the #1 person on their mind at that moment! Let the person catch your enthusiasm right from the start. While the programmed robot says a dull "Hello," the enthusiast answers with a cheery "Good afternoon" or even "With a little good news for you, this could be both of our days." Surprise the caller right from the start. Develop new enthusiastic ways of answering the phone every day by letting your creativity flow. Your opening words on the phone are limited only by your creativity.

6. Listen to others enthusiastically. Win people over by listening enthusiastically. As you listen to people talk, lean forward, nodding your head, eager for the next word. Use open, expressive eyes, conveying full attentiveness to the speaker's ideas. The world's best salespeople are not only great, enlivening speakers with positive vocabularies but enthusiastic listeners as well. Stay away from playing games like "Can you top this?" or "That reminds me of my experience. Let me tell you about it." Stay on the speaker's topic and watch your popularity soar!

What are you most enthusiastic about in life right now? What's good and new in your life?

_____

_____

How else can get you more out of each moment? Psychologists tell us to become more mindful of each moment.

3. Be MINDFUL (Aware of your Experiences)

Psychologists are discovering an exciting approach to more fulfilled living they are calling "Mindfulness." Mindfulness is a fuller awareness of our present experience with acceptance. Mindfulness involves being present and fully attentive, digging deeper into "the now." When we are mindful, our attention

> *Mindfulness is a fuller awareness of our present experience with acceptance.*

is neither caught up in past events, nor engaged in planning or worrying about the future. Psychologist Christopher Germer defines mindfulness as having (1) a fuller awareness of (2) our present experiences with (3) acceptance. Being mindful involves allowing more of the moment to simply be "as-is" through all of your five senses as well as your moment-to-moment experiences! Feel it, taste it, hear it, see it, smell it. Allow more of the present possibilities to expose themselves to your senses. Notice common things in your everyday experiences that you didn't see before and dig deeper sensually to sense more. It involves staying where you are, without forcing new experiences or getting away from the present or drifting to the past or future. Mindfulness is being in touch with the present, the here and now to your raw experiencing, as well as any other awareness, however fleeting. When you are mindful, you are really living in the moment.

In his book *Full Catastrophe Living,* John Kabat-Zinn defines mindfulness as "Moment-to-moment awareness, which is cultivated by purposefully paying attention to things we ordinarily never give a moment's thought to. More specifically mindfulness is said to lead to the development of new kinds of control and wisdom in our lives, based on our inner capacities for relaxation, paying attention, awareness, and insight. Mindfulness is being still to experience a rich awareness of now!!"

Liz, a Calgary, Canada stylist told me, "I remember when I would come home from school and my mom would have rearranged the same old living room furniture in new ways. The couch would be in a different part of the room, the chairs were moved, the pictures were put in different places. It was fun, like we had a new house. She rearranged the same old furniture to make it look new. Didn't cost a penny. So I decided that, on occasion, I would do the same thing in the salon.

Then I discovered something even more stimulating. It is so exciting to look at the same old areas of the salon in a new way, hear sounds I'd never heard before. Sense odors that were not present to me before but may have been to our clients. And even to be more aware of how my touch felt to my clients, and myself, especially during the shampooing." Whether Liz knew it or not, she was becoming more mindful. She brought all of her senses to the party of the moment!

When we are being mindful, we don't need to "get away" or travel to a new country, take a walk on a sandy beach or climb a mountain to be refreshed. We can "get away" by "getting into" the moment. We rearrange our "living" room furniture, in our mind. We become more "aware" by becoming more "still." Start by being mindful, that is, more sensually aware of your present experiences with acceptance of what is fully there both outside and inside you in the moment.

Again, we have all we need when we are being mindful. We are present, rather than absent, in the moment. Mindfulness involves becoming more aware of your experiences, by heightening your feelings, sights, sounds, tastes, and scents. Take a few minutes to develop your mindfulness. Experience this moment without judgment; only bring your five senses to it.

4. Put Yourself into a State of FLOW (Finding Deeper Meaning in Your Work)

When we are mindful, we are more sensually aware and accepting of the moment. Another approach to getting more out of an experience is to dig deeper into whatever we are engaged in, in the outside world at any given moment. This is "Flow." Flow involves rearranging the contents of your conscious mind in such a way as to create meaning. Being in a state of flow involves being totally mentally absorbed in a task. Flow is the experience of finding deeper or higher meaning in any experience and is more mental than the more sensual state of being mindful.

Did you ever have a moment when you felt so naturally high, so ecstatic, so

> *Flow involves rearranging the contents of your conscious mind in such a way as to create meaning.*

appreciative, that you were overcome with great joy? Psychologist Mihaly Csikzentmihalyi describes these special moments as moments of "Flow." He writes that, "Happiness is the state of being totally absorbed in a task. This is when we are in a state of flow. Flow improves the quality of that experience and provides enjoyment, concentration and involvement. When in flow, the sense of time and self-consciousness disappears as we experience ourselves breaking out of previous boundaries."

He adds, "Flow is the state of being so absorbed in an activity that nothing else seems to matter. The immersion in the experience itself takes the focus away from self-consciousness and outside problems. Curiously, happiness is not something that happens or something that power can command. It does not depend upon outside events, but rather how we interpret them. Happiness is a condition that ought to be prepared for and cultivated by each of us privately. People who learn to control their inner experiences are able to determine the quality of their lives."

How can you put yourself into a state of flow at work? Start by rearranging the contents of your conscious mind in such a way as to create deeper meaning in your artistry and its impact on peoples' lives. Take any salon experience and "see" new meaning in it. The power of flow is available to you if you are will-ing.

Lena had both a mindful and flow experience one morning. First Lena was sensually mindful when commuting to her Washington DC salon while observing the first appearance of the cherry blossoms one Spring day. She smelled and saw sensually the beauty of the processes of nature. Then, as her very first client's hair was processing her color she chilled up realizing she was a part of the process... not on a tree, but on a person. Here in her own work, in her same salon she'd been in a thousand times, she was in the state of flow!

5. Take Time to Appreciate What You Already Have

Today is a dream you'll have in your future. Twenty years from now you'll wish you were back where you are today, twenty years younger than you will be. So grab it now while you can. You have everything you need. You are alive. You have today. Your life is now.

1. Appreciating your family. What was the best thing that each of your family members has done for you. Someone cooked for you as you were growing up, someone worked for you to get you clothes and an education. Maybe others were there for you during challenging times. Re-appreciate your family and write each one a nice note of thanks.

2. Appreciating your friends. Who is your best friend? What are some of the special things he or she did for you? Thank him or her for being there for you through the years.

3. Appreciating your profession. Do you remember the day you first saw your name on your cosmetology license? The first time you realized you were a professional stylist. How exciting! You can "re-new" that same excitement today by looking at your license – that you earned. And your state or province has given you the credentials to touch and design peoples' self-images. Appreciate your salon chair that you saw people grow up in. Appreciate your professional tools, shears, brushes, perm rods, etc.

4. Appreciating your clients. Who is your favorite client? Why? Which client's hairstyle have you changed the most? How did the person feel? Appreciate each of the clients who chose you – and your salon – over all other salons in your area. Let every person know you don't take him or her for granted.

5. Appreciating your teammates. Appreciate the salon owner or manager for believing in you and giving you an opportunity in the salon. Appreciate the stylist you are closest with in the salon today. With which other teammates have you shared both good and bad moments?

You can spend today re-living that tough client from yesterday, and go through the fire twice. Or you can fully live this new momentum. As it is. Stop waiting for the better days of the future to arrive. You'll never be this young again, and you've never had so much wisdom. These are the good times. So don't take today for granted...because it is the only day that you really have now! Appreciate today.

Tips to Love Life

1. Remind yourself from time to time that you are alive. And being alive gives you unlimited opportunities to shape your day. Even when feeling down, your emotions tell you that you are alive, and being alive gives you hope.

2. Experience how much you could accomplish in a moment. In an hour. In a day. In a year. In a lifetime.

3. Be mindful. Get into this moment fully with each of your five senses. How does each one sound, look, feel, even how does it smell and taste? Dig deeper into each moment.

4. Put yourself into a state of flow. Arrange the contents of your conscious mind in such a way as to create deeper meaning in your work experiences.

5. Develop your enthusiasm for your life and your day. Ask yourself enthusiastic questions. For example:

   "What special thing am I going to do for someone right now?"

   "What can I do right now to make myself one step better?"

   "What work needs to get done? How can I fully engross myself in that task?"
   "Who do I know that needs cheering up?"

6. Appreciate some of the things you do have, rather than take them for granted. Love your life!

If you've found these ideas meaningful, consider reading the book *Flow* by Mihaly Csikszentmihalyi.

For any questions, further dialogue, or challenges with material in this chapter, please email us at howardh@peoplemediainc.com.

Chapter 6
Be Driven from Within

Not only are you alive, but you are the only person who chooses the attitude you will take towards today. The secret to life is to understand that happiness and success are inside us, and if we are driven from within, life will be on your side! As our friend Bert Jacobs tells us with his inspiring concept, "Life is Good!"

Psy-Cosmetologists have an overall love of life, and they are driven from within as they face each day's challenges. "Nothing is stronger than my attitude," Glen from a little Texas city told me. "I'd rather have a great attitude facing tough challenges than have a poor attitude with no challenges," Brenda asserted. She captured the general attitude of the Psy-Cosmetologists throughout the world. These self-determined salon professionals aren't afraid of the future because they have all they need; they are alive, and they choose to bring an upbeat attitude with them as they view their challenges as opportunities dressed in work clothes. This takes inner drive. Inner drive is the experience of being motivated from within.

> *Inner drive is the experience of being motivated from within.*

What are some ways you can build your inner drive?

1. Use Your #1 Tool for Happiness: Your Winning Attitude!

2. Stop Blaming and Start Living

3. Discover the Power of Rational Thinking

4. Develop Your Inner Security

1. Use Your #1 Tool for Happiness: Your Winning Attitude!

I respectfully disagree with many of my fellow psychologists whose work was often based upon studies with pigeons and dogs, who conclude that we, like the other animals, are just helpless responders to our environments. In other words some psychologists, and many people believe that for our lives to improve we need something "out there in the environment," to change to make our lives better. To this way of thinking I argue that waiting for my outside world to change before I change is like looking into a mirror at my reflection, and saying to my reflection, "if you move first, I'll move!" There is a better way. If I move, my reflection in my environment will move. Yes, we do have an animal nature conditioned by our past, but we have something else... our human nature that allows us to choose our attitude that we take through our lives.

It is in our human nature, and in our attitude where we find our freedom. Through our attitude we can transcend our past, our circumstances, our anxieties, our habits, and sometimes even our illnesses and creatively design a new destiny for ourselves. Through our human nature we can dream, imagine, plan, think, create, invent, determine, and decide whether to take ourselves to the left or right, and up or down. The philosopher Bertrand Russell concluded that in the vast realm of the alive, creative human mind, there are no limitations. Our only limitation is time.

We have to decide which attitude we will bring to each game day of life. We can choose to continue to be shaped by our animal nature. Or we can choose to transcend our animal nature and move from our creative human nature. That is why some of us survive living out of our animal nature, rarely straying from our safe neighborhoods, while others, moving from our higher human nature, walk on the moon.

The visionaries, driven by their human nature go forward eagerly, into the unknown, strengthened by their own inner security foundation. To the conditioned animal, anxiety, or uncertainty is a signal to retreat. But to the fully functioning, self-actualizing human, anxiety is a motivating signal like the gun at the starting line of a race, to conquer some of life's uncertainties. Hasn't every great achievement in your life been preceded by great amounts of anxiety?

And to those who say that we are helpless products of our environments, I caution that there has never been one study that showed a perfect relationship between the things that happened to us in our pasts as being the direct cause of our choices today. Not one.

Today you choose to either live from your animal nature and be a product of your environment. Or, as a Psy-Cosmetologist to start living from your higher human nature... and make your environment be a product of your determination. What will determine your day and destiny- your environment, or your attitude?

Physically speaking, our resource is our bodies. Socially speaking, our resources are our friends. Financially speaking our resources are our assets. Spiritually speaking, our resource is our God. And motivationally speaking, our resource is our attitude. In fact, you could say that we are our attitude.

Our attitude is the best predictor of the results we will experience today. Our attitude either gives us more power to deal with the challenges we face. Or we can create even more misery for ourselves.

Our attitude toolbox is our thoughts, our emotions and our actions, which together form our attitude.

Our Attitude Toolbox

Our Thoughts + Our Emotions + Our Actions = Our Attitude

We can change our attitude by either changing our thoughts, our feelings or our actions. You might remember in Chapter 6 when we learned that a way to feel enthusiastic was to start acting enthusiastic. For many people, however, the easiest way of creating a better attitude is by thinking about things differently. When we ***think*** about things differently, or see things in new ways, we start to ***feel*** differently and are more likely to act differently. For example, if I dwell on the crises I face in the salon, I can make myself angry or depressed. But if I assume that my work will have challenges, and I expect them, then I feel motivated to drive over these bumps. My new ***thoughts*** can change my ***feelings*** and my ***actions***.

Our thoughts are real things. They are as solid as bricks. And like bricks, thoughts can build great dreams or they can destroy great dreams. Our thoughts will either give us inner power, or get us discouraged by giving our power away to the outside world.

Your Attitude Vantage Point Determines How Far You Can See

Creative human minds and passionate human hearts have produced achievements that only days before had been viewed as impossible. What is possible is being revised daily through people stretching the human will and spirit. Humans with a "can-do" attitude have climbed to the highest points on the earth and instead of wringing their hands over problems were determined to face their challenges and soar to new heights. No doubt, in your own life, when you faced challenges in beauty school, you felt the goal of your license in your pumping heart and found ways of getting it done. It was all in your attitude. You said, "yes," rather than "no," to life.

As I wished happy holidays to two women I had know for 40 years, one pushing a shopping cart, the other riding in it in the aisle of our local market, I was inspired by the fun they were having together. The twins were conjoined at the heads at birth and were living largely on their own for almost five decades. Their attitude was stronger than their challenges. They went forward with a smile on their face.

Only moments later in the same market's parking lot, I witnessed two honking drivers cursing at each others with words and gestures over whose saw the space first. They continued yelling at each other on this Christmas Eve as they walked into the market.

If you want to ask if the #1 tool for living is your attitude, ask the two girls, not the two guys.

Some choose to see their lives as an overwhelming series of dreary events. These hand-wringers can take you down quickly by arguing that the world is against them, and you, by pointing out all of the injustices and the challenges of our times.

Its true that we may not have as much, or be as lucky as, or as beautiful as some others who have power, fame and beauty. We may not be the North American Hairdresser of the Year or the styling director of the major company. But, in the end, whether we sleep in a $50,000 dollar a night home on an island or on the humble bed we lie in at home each night, we have a lot in common: we have to choose the attitude we will take with us as we meet our life experiences.

Our attitude is the greatest treasure we have. And, maybe, the only one we need. Prove that you can use your attitude to deal with something that is now upsetting you.

2. Stop Blaming and Start Living

We give our power away to whatever we blame! You have you! And you have now! How will you use your now? To find things in your outer world to blame, or to find ways in your inner world to build? Your tomorrow is determined by your decisions today, isn't it?

One California Psy-Cosmetologist wrote me about my book *If It Weren't for You, We Could Get Along!*. The email read:

"These ideas in this book cleared my mind of its loud noises. I can think again. I can feel alive again! I can do something, even if I can't do everything. I got it – Dr. Lew's message – early in the book, and it hit me like a warm, refreshing spring breeze after a frozen winter. My past, my boss, my job, my ex, the nasty weather, the traffic jams, the stock market, and even the terrorists are no longer going to live rent free in my mind. I have to get back to living, because that's what life is for. The only thing I wonder about is how could ideas so sensible and so powerful be so simple and clear! And how could **one single change in me** produce such a positive effect on my life?

The underlined words in her letter proved that she "got it." What is there to "get?"

Finding the Single Factor Leading to Personal Growth and Happiness

Psychotherapists observe a common pattern present in the first session with almost every client. Through therapy, one major change takes place. When therapy is successful, therapists note how the last session differs from the first. It can be whittled down to one new approach to life that the client has taken. In the first session, the helpless, frustrated, anxious, hurt or angry client unfolds a litany of people and things that they are spending their time blaming for their frenzied emotional state. It might be, "The manager made me mad," or, "My 9 o'clock is never happy with the cut I give her and it depresses me."

The major change? By the last session, usually none of these outside people or things in the world have changed, but the person has changed. The client has transformed herself, by deciding to build her inner world, rather than to blame their outer world.

I decided that it was important to cut through the many hours of agreeing with the appropriateness of the blame, with the resultant anger, hurt, pain, etc. Oh, I empathized that if that was the way they felt, they had every right to feel that way – even unto their dying days and beyond. It was their choice. I did talk to them about people who had made uplifting and constructive decisions to build. Among these people was my friend Rosalie Bailey, who, despite having cerebral palsy and just a fourth grade education, made the single choice to stop blaming the outer world and start building her inner world. She went on to earn three college degrees and inspire a group of people to build America's largest professional beauty company. She certainly had every right to spend her short life blaming, but she decided to live rather than to blame.

The single most empowering decision that will change your life is to get over making the outside world so important. Start building your inside world. Move forward. It will take the same amount of time – that is, this moment – to start reconstructing your future as it would to helplessly use it up blaming. You can build yourself. It starts with your decision to stop blaming. Why does blaming hold us back? Because we give our power away to whatever we take the time to blame. The happiest, healthiest, self-actualizing human beings stop blaming their outer world and start building their inner selves.

Listen for the "If It Weren't For...s"

Take a few seconds and think about the people near you at home or at work. What are the things or the people that they blame for making their life miserable?

• Other people

• The past

• Fears and weaknesses

• No confidence and lack of support from others

• Reality

• The people in the workplace

• The huge challenge ahead

These may range from other people to events in their past. Or they may even be blaming their own fears, lack of confidence, bad luck, limited education, or pessimism for holding them back.

Listen carefully for the reasons why they can't be more, do more, sell more, and life more. Listen for their, "If it weren't for...s"

"If it weren't for_____, _____, _____, _____, etc., I could be happy!"

What are you blaming and giving your power away to? Become determined to stop giving your power away to it!

3. Discover the Power of Rational Thinking

Two of the most significant people of the past century who helped us realize our "reasoning power" were psychiatrist Alfred Adler, and psychologist Albert Ellis. Adler, in the early part of the century, concluded that neither heredity nor environment determine us. They are just the building blocks that we construct to design ourselves. When we blame, we act "as if" we live in a faulty building and we can't do anything about it until the builder comes back, apologizes, and rebuilds us a mansion. Then we could be happy.

Albert Ellis is founder of Rational Thinking eventually calling it Rational-Emotive- Behavioral Therapy (REBT) and co-author of the life-changing *A New Guide to Rational Living*. Ellis is one of the leading thinkers of the last century, argued that life is as simple as A-B-C. I had the pleasure of studying with Albert Ellis.

The ABC's of Rational Thinking

How can you make use of the systematic process of Rational Thinking to help you in the salon, and in life? Its as easy as A-B-C.

Imagine a typical experience we may face in life. Somebody rams into the back of our new car. We aren't injured but we know our car needs serious work. Traumatic? Well, that depends on how well we know our ABC's.

Ellis calls those challenging events in life Activating Events, or the A's in the ABC's of rational thinking. When the back of our car is hit, it activates our mind to think about the event.

So at "A" we put "someone ran into the back of my car"

At "C" is our Consequent Emotion, which is how we are feeling. For example, "anger at the driver who hit us"

Before Ellis, most people thought "A", the **A**ctivating Event, automatically caused "C," our Consequent Emotion. And very few people would question that it was the activating event, the crash, that causes our consequent emotion, anger.

Ellis would then ask us, "If 1,000 people all have the back of their cars hit, would all 1,000 people have the same amount of anger, or even be angry? Would some even check to see if the driver who hit them is OK? Consider the

huge variety of reactions to the same event.

One person might get out of the car, get the insurance and drivers license, take the necessary pictures, file an accident report and get the car fixed. No anger, **just taking action to solve the problem**.

Another person experiencing the same event might be **frustrated** that he won't have his car for a few weeks, and start shouting at the driver, "Don't you know how to drive, you idiot?" He might even continue ranting and raving for fifteen more minutes. After his show is over, then what does he have to do? Get the other driver's insurance information and get the car fixed. The anger ADDED nothing, but TOOK AWAY 30 minutes of his life!

And maybe a third person would be so **angry** he would jump out of his car with his fists up, takes an hour, threatens the driver, gets in an argument with the police, and then what does he still have to do? You got it! Get the insurance information and get the car fixed.

The fact that there were three different reactions at "C" proves that the things that happen to us at "A," or the Activating Events, are not the cause of our **C**onsequent Emotions at "C." The question than becomes, "if our experiences don't directly determine our emotions, than what is the cause of our feelings?

In my opinion you are about learn the most important insight in the history of psychology. Ellis called it "Rational Thinking."

Rational Thinking argues that the real cause of our emotions at "C," is not the things that happen to us at "A," but rather our **B**eliefs, or what we tell ourselves at "B."

So, in order to understand our emotions, here are the A-B-C's of Rational Thinking.

Activating Event "A"	**B**eliefs "B"	**C**onsequent Emotions "C"
We fail a test	"The test wasn't fair"	**Anger** at the teacher
	OR	
We fail a test	"I'm stupid and worthless"	**Depression**, feeling **inadequate**
	OR	
We fail a test	"I didn't put the right answers in the right places this time. I have to study harder next time."	**Determination** to study harder in the future

Get it? Just as you are what you eat, you are what you believe. Memorize the ABC's of Rational Thinking and practice them every opportunity you get. You will find yourself being able to re-route any event you experience. Things that at one time in your life might have bent you out of shape emotionally will have no power over you. You'll discover that, in the end, it is your beliefs that affect you. Not your experiences.

Think of a feeling you are having today that you wished you weren't experiencing. That is "C". Now look at what you are saying caused it at "A". What are you telling yourself at "B" that is causing your upsetted mind at "C"? Try different things to tell yourself at "B". Can you affect your feelings at "C", perhaps even using humor?

_____

_____

4. Develop Your Inner Security

Our inner security shows in our ability to trust ourselves, even in the absence of outside approval and praise. Here is a question we could ask about inner security:

"What would we do, if from this moment onward, for the rest of our life no one ever, anywhere again approved of us or our actions, applauded us, or even said, "Good job?"

Would we still survive? Would we really start doubting ourselves? Would we crave approval? Would we become weaker and less secure by the day?

Or would we start finding strengths inside ourselves to keep us going forward? Would we start finding ways to reinforce ourselves? If so, then we would be developing our inner security.

Is our security foundation inside, or outside us? We need to get our foundation of support and motivation from some source. And the source can be in our environment, or it can be within ourselves. (This, of course, is in addition to our spiritual foundation). Unfortunately most people look for their security, sometimes with obsession from outside sources, rather than constructing their own solid permanent foundation to stand on. Here are a few general things to remember about inner security:

1. When our security is outside us, we need to be pushed, pulled, praised and applauded by others.

2. When our security is inside us, we are driven by inner sources and we function just as effectively when we don't receive the positive push from the outside world.

3. When our security is on the outside we become higher maintenance to

others, constantly needing them to approve of our work and maybe even our human worth.

4. When our security is inside us we have an internal point of evaluation and can correct, reinforce and improve ourselves.

Externally secure people sometimes aren't even sure how they feel about things until someone else tells them. They look for clues in the outside world. When an externally secure person is asked if he is hungry, he doesn't simply reflect inside and conclude, "yes," or "no" – he has to check his cell phone to see what time it is. The clock knows better if he is hungry than he does! When our security is in the outside world, we are constantly preoccupied with thoughts like, "Does everyone like me?"

It's nice to be liked, but outside approval leaves us with ups and downs like the rise and fall of the stock market each day. Psy-Cosmetologists know there is a better way – inner security. The general rule is that the more inner security people have, the less outer predictability they need from the outside. Inner secure people are driven by their own inner sources and forces. Their evaluation point is inside themselves. The advantage here is that they will always have their security, because they will always have themselves.

Despite being a young stylist, Melinda had great inner security. She had a good feel for what a great cut was, and had the inner security to trust herself. She also knew that some people will compliment every style she does, while others will never be satisfied (you'll learn more about this passive-aggressive style later). Because of her inner sense of trust when someone compliments a look she gives that Melinda herself doesn't quite feel right about, Melinda still suggests ways of making little improvements. On the other hand, when a person who is never satisfied complains, Melinda looks at the style, likes it and reassures her client.

Melinda then doesn't go home at night putting herself down because one of her ten clients wasn't happy.

Develop your inner security by trusting yourself, making recommendations from your professional wisdom and technical skills. And when someone is unhappy with your work, ask yourself, "Could I improve this style or look?" If so, improve it. If not, reassure the client that she may like it if she lives with it for a few days.

Tips to Be Driven from Within

1. Experience the power of your attitude. Change your attitude and you'll change your life.

2. Stop blaming and start living. When you catch yourself blaming the outside world and getting yourself upset, stop, pause and remind yourself that the thing that is causing your frustration is how you are looking at the situation.

3. Prove that you can deal with anything through Rational Thinking. Your beliefs

at "B" not the event at "A" is the part you have control over. Remember again that it is not what happens to you that is the cause, but your beliefs are the cause of your emotions. When you use this method, feel pride in mastering Rational Thinking.

4. Start viewing yourself as the greatest agent of change in your life. When your security foundation is inside you, you can deal with outside challenges because you can give yourself your own pat on the back. You've got you!

If you've found these ideas meaningful, consider reading the book *If It Weren't For You, We Could Get Along!* by Lewis Losoncy.

For any questions, further dialogue, or challenges with material in this chapter, please email us at howardh@peoplemediainc.com.

Chapter 7
Change People's Lives

You are alive! You choose the attitude you face the world with today. And you are driven from within. You have everything you need. Plus, remember that each day in the salon you are changing the world.

In addition to being both enthusiastic about life and self-motivated, Psy-Cosmetologists inspire themselves by realizing their positive influence on their clients' lives. They know each of their clients, their likes and dislikes, their joys and anxieties. In consultations with their clients, Psy-Cosmetologists consider the psychological factors, such as personality (introvert or extrovert), change comfort level, and lifestyle. For example, they wouldn't give twin sisters, with the same hair and bone structure, the same look, because they are different people. One might be a creative artist who thrives on change, and the other might be a conservative banker.

Because of their great communication skills that open people up to share, Psy-Cosmetologists are aware of a person's important future life events.

"We can start planning for your new look for your daughter Cassandra's wedding. If you see some looks you'd like to talk about considering, bring them with you, Michelle," one aware Midwestern salon artist suggests.

While some stylists think of their clients impersonally as "9 o'clocks," or "walk-ins," or "my color service," Psy-Cosmetologists experience each client uniquely, and will have thoughts like, "Here comes Emily, who loves her looks to fit perfectly with her new outfits," or "Savannah, who will be in later today, is up for anything."

As you can see, having a higher people purpose adds human value to their work, and fulfills Psy-Cosmetologists' social and inspirational needs, as well as their financial ones. They spend the same amount of time in the salon as other stylists, but get so many more rewards because of experiencing their impact on people. Not just on their hair, skin or nails. You could say they are client-centered, not self-centered.

What are some ways of changing peoples' lives?

1. Realize the Human Significance of Your Work

2. Bring Both Your Style and Sensitivity

3. Have a Positive Impact on Your Community

4. Sense Opportunities to Make Someone Feel Special

1. Realize the Human Significance of Your Work

Psy-Cosmetologists create so many more rewards for themselves in their work. They believe that they don't just change hair, skin and nails. They have a higher, human view of their work. They change peoples' lives!

"I have a lady who wouldn't dream of going out to a party without first coming in to see me," one Oregon stylist told me. She laughed and added, "One week she came in twice. I told her she doesn't really need anything but she insisted that she just feels better being here.

It gives her confidence." Imagine, cosmetically she was fine. She needed a lift in another way.

An example of the importance of creating a human purpose to your work is told in a little story Colin Walsh and I wrote about in our book, *ON: A Brilliant Way to Live and Work.*

Three Men at Work

Three men were out in the field tilling the soil.

A person passed by and stopped and asked the first man, "What are you doing?" He responded, "I'm tilling the soil."

The curious stranger turned to the second man, asking him the same question. Without hesitation he answered, "What am I doing? I'm making a living."

When he finally got the third man's attention and asked what he was doing, the tiller paused, smiled, and responded, "I'm feeding the community!"

While all three worked the same amount of time, in the same field, doing the same amount of work, the first person's days seemed longer than the second man's days. The third man so loved his work that he wasn't aware of the time.

Near the end of their lives, the first man thought his while lifetime work was meaningless. The second man said he was able to feed his family through his work. But, the third man felt very peaceful because he lived an inspired life by making the world a better place doing his lifework.

They were all doing the same work.

Because Psy-Cosmetologists experience the human impact of their work on others, they add value to the professional products and services and to themselves as professionals. Some people go to work to make money to pay bills, while others are "turned on" to their work.

Consider this special salon owner who helped her staff to realize the importance of their work:

"If you want to do hair, you can work anywhere. If you want to change people's lives by realizing that you are giving them courage, confidence and hope through your skills in styling and coloring, then we would be honored to have you working with our salon family. As a salon artist, you are in one of only five professions that touches people, along with the doctor, dentist, nurse and massage therapist. You will be touching your clients' lives anywhere from six to fifty times a year, more frequently than they see their relatives. And you have the skills and tools to make them beautiful. Can you imagine a more important gift than that? That's what you will be doing here at our salon."

"Having been a hairdresser for years, I moved from salon to salon based on the amount of commission I would get. But after listening to Carmen speak, I found a new type of reward, a different type of paycheck Carmen would give. I was inspired for the first time in my life to touch people's lives in a more meaningful way!" Carmen helped her staff realize the human significance of their work.

Describe a client whose life you have helped and influenced. What did you do? What did he or she do or say as a result?

_____

_____

2. Bring Both Your Style and Sensitivity

Psy-Cosmetologists ceremoniously celebrate the child's first cut, often taking a picture of that precious moment, and placing the hair into an envelope or special place to hold it. Proms and wedding days are important emotional times in the lives of sensitive stylists who consciously "liven things up" for their clients. It is especially touching to experience how important the sensitive Psy-Cosmetologist is in the lives of her clients. You can imagine how the lifelong sensitivity of a Psy-Cosmetologist can be most important in their greying days.

A Tom's River, New Jersey, salon-owner husband-and-wife team shared, "The reason the elderly act like they have so much going for them and frustrated when we make them wait is because the very opposite is quite often true. Unfortunately, some believe they have very little going for them, but they don't want us to know it. They want us to think of them as first- class, not second-class, citizens, and they are. So even before they say something to us, in our salon we tell them, "I know how busy you are Mr. or Mrs._____, so we'll get to you as soon as possible." We communicate our respect for them.

Rumor has it that the elderly flock to this kind of salon. That's an example of Psy-Cosmetology in action.

A poem was written by an elderly patient in a London hospital that best expresses some of the frustrations many senior citizens experience after living a life of being active, competent, and capable, and then finding themselves one day victims of the aging process. Although it was written to a nurse, we'd like to change a few words to have it apply to the salon. (The original author of the poem remains anonymous.)

A Poem on Loneliness

What do you see, stylist, what do you see?
What are you thinking when you are looking at me,
A crabby old woman, not very wise,
Uncertain of habit, with faraway eyes,
Who is late for appointments and makes no reply,
When you say in a loud voice, "I do wish you'd try!"

I'll tell you who I am as I sit here so still,
As I rise at your bidding and I lift my head at your will.
I'm a small child of ten with a father and a mother,
With brothers and sisters who love one another.
A bride soon at twenty my heart gives a leap,
Remembering the vows I promised to keep.

At twenty-five now I have young of my own,
Who need me to build a secure and happy home.
At fifty once more babies round my knee,
Again we knew children, my loved one and me.

Dark days are upon me, my husband is dead.
I look to the future, I shudder with dread,
And I think of the years and the love that I've known.

I'm an old woman now and nature is cruel,
'Tis her jest to make old age look like a fool.
This body it crumbles, grace and vigor depart,
There now is a stone where I once had a heart.

But inside this carcass a young girl still dwells,
And now and again my bittered heart swells.
I remember the joys, I remember the pain,
I'm living and loving all over again.

And I think of the years all too few gone too fast,
And accept the stark fact that nothing will last.
So open your eyes, stylist, open and see,
Not a crabby old 9' o clock, look closer, see me.

How important is her sensitive stylist to her? Who else in the world cares about her? Who knows her better than her hairdresser? And chances are that the stylist is one of the rare human contacts this woman has on a regular basis.

Can you think of any elderly clients whom you enjoy working with a lot or who you have influenced in some way? Describe him or her.

_____

_____

3. Have a Positive Impact on the Community

The prime example of a true Psy-Cosmetologist was Peggy Eason of Battle Creek, Iowa. Peggy asked if I would come to Battle Creek to talk to the people in her town.

"Dr Lew, you must come to Battle Creek to talk on positive attitudes the next time you are in the area."

"I'd love to, Peggy. About how big is Battle Creek?"

"Oh, we have over 800 people now," the attractive, enthusiastic salon owner proudly stated.

"Well, Peggy," I cautiously replied, "with 800 people, don't get your expectations up too high. Let's shoot for maybe a dozen people or so to be at our talk."

"Oh no, Dr. Lew! We'll have a lot more than that! A hairstylist touches a lot of lives who touch a lot of lives of other people."

The talk was arranged, and four months later Peggy, one of her stylists, and I drove from Des Moines to Battle Creek. By this time, Peggy had quite a full schedule prepared for me. She pulled out a slip of paper and reviewed my itinerary – "At 9:00 we have a radio program on the importance of hairdressers. At 10:00 you'll be with the newspaper. At 1:00 you'll be with all of the high school students of Battle Creek, at 2:30 with all of the schoolteachers, and at 7:30 you'll speak in the high school gym to the people of Battle Creek." Peggy's goal was to raise money from admission fees to help get a new ambulance for the community. The day went really well! The people of Battle Creek, Iowa from student to bank teller to disc jockey to waitress, were all gracious.

The Power of One Psy-Cosmetologist in Her Community

Finally, the evening arrived. As I prepared my notes for the talk in the football coach's office, no less than the school superintendent came to the door and said, "Peggy is ready for you." As I walked out on the gym floor expecting twenty or twenty-five people, I saw every seat in the bleachers filled and the sides of the room loaded with additional seats to accommodate the overflow. I looked on to the gym floor, and holding a microphone to introduce me was the stylist-owner of Nu Fashion Salon of Battle Creek.

Peggy made her public speaking debut by introducing me to over 400 of her fellow citizens. Half of the town! Peggy made her contribution to the community. She reached out to others. Through the efforts of a hairstylist, hundreds of lives were touched, the ambulance came closer to being a reality, and the town took one giant step towards understanding the power of a Psy-Cosmetologist! Peggy is a true professional who wants to do her part to help her community become a better place.

Have there been times you or your salon made your community better? What are some things you could do to help your community?

_____

_____

4. Changing Lives by Sensing Opportunities to Make Someone Feel Special

Your services are a treat. They are special experiences for people. Two Michigan salon owners, Nikki in Kalamazoo and Kim in Grand Rapids both held staff motivation days in which they also invited in other salons from their areas.

Curiously, Psy-Cosmetologists take a higher view by not thinking of other salons as their competition, but rather as people who share the dreams of making a better world from behind the chair. Part of what their staffs did was to go to a local woman's shelter and offer their salon services to some women who were experiencing challenges in their lives. The women were offered an hour of motivation to build their inner self-image and then, more importantly, three hours with the salon stylists and specialists to build their outer image. You might say that their total image was affected by this special day Nikki and Kim's salon teams offered.

One dynamic stylist Erin observed that she saw her client changed dramatically during that special day. Another woman was studying to be a minister. During that day she confided in this stylist – whom she had just met – about her excitements and anxieties that she hadn't shared with anyone before. The professionals in these two salons sensed opportunities to help these important women to feel how special they are.

Franki Anderson of Franki and Co. and her staff hold a fund-raiser every year for breast cancer awareness for the people of Tri-Counties in Eastern Washington. Setting a goal of 100,000 dollars for the cause makes it the event of the year for the community. The people of Richland and the Tri-County area lucky to have a caring staff. Their salon's clientele extends throughout the States of Washington, Idaho and Oregon.

Think of the 3 year-old, the 6 year-old in your chair for the first day of school, the 15 year-old cheerleader wearing your hair under the Friday night football fields lights, the prom night girl sharing her anxieties, the wedding day look, and all of the other important events of life. All of these stories are heard from your chair. As one Missouri hairdresser asked me, "What is it about that chair?"

Think of three clients who you are going to make feel special. What will you do?

_____

_____

_____

_____

_____

Tips to Change People's Lives

1. Constantly remind yourself that, "This is a person, not a mannequin, in my chair. And she returns to our salon because we are having an impact on her life."

2. Remember that it is not just your style that touches your client. It is also your sensitivity with her.

3. Think big. How can your salon offer your professional gifts to make your neighborhood or city a better place?

4. Who will you make special today?

If you've found these ideas meaningful, consider reading the book *On: A Brilliant Way to Live & Work* by Lewis Losoncy and Colin Walsh.

For any questions, further dialogue, or challenges with material in this chapter, please email us at howardh@peoplemediainc.com.

Chapter 8
Be Open to Grow

You are alive! You choose your attitude today. And you are in a profession that changes peoples' lives. Plus, being alive when you are open to grow allows the whole world to open itself up for you.

Psy-Cosmetologists are highly motivated salon artists who are aware of the life- changing power in being open to new ideas for growth. While some stylists painfully arrive at educational events only to get their hours to meet the requirements of the state, Psy-Cosmetologists are excited to find better ways of living and working.

Psy-Cosmetologists are highly motivated self-starters who are driven from within, not needing to be pushed by the outside world to perform. They love learning and seriously consider every education program, knowing it will pay off in the big picture. They take charge and look for opportunities in every experience.

"The toughest challenge I ever faced was when my sales consultant forced me to go to a class where I discovered how behind the times I was," Mary from Ohio explained. "My eyes were opened because I let these new ideas in and it started paying off. One day of education started me on a journey to see things more clearly and learn everything I could, and we turned our salon around. I'm not saying it was easy, but it was well worth it!" Mary opened up her mind, took responsibility for her growth and built her salon.

When you think about it, when we are open, the whole world opens itself up for us to grow from. And when we are closed, we block out all the rich powers and ideas of the universe that could refresh us and actualize us. In fact, if you want to predict if a person will be more actualized tomorrow than today, simply observe how open the person is to let new ideas, new ways of looking at things, and new people into her world.

What are some ways you will be growing in this chapter?

1. Discover Yourself through the Johari Window

2. Choose to Be Growth-Centered, Not Self-Centered

3. Become a Criticism Welcomer

4. Rise above Comparison Thinking

Let's start with the dynamic concept of the Johari Window.

1. Discover Yourself through the Johari Window

Psychologists Joseph Luft and Harry Ingram developed a concept to help people become more aware of their Open and Closed areas. The Johari Window is a strategy to increase one's self-awareness. Let's take a look at the Johari Window.

> ## *The Johari Window is a way of measuring one's self-awareness.*

	Known to Self	Not Known to Self
Known to Others	1 Not Open	2 Blind Spot
Not Known to Others	3 Hidden	4 Unknown

The JoHari Windows reveals four areas of awareness.

Window 1 is our Open Area. In our Open Area of awareness we see things that we know about ourselves that others also see. This might be our eye color, our everyday personality and things that we are conscious of that we leave out there for the world to see. The more Open Areas we have, the less defensive we are. Self-actualizing people are constantly expanding their Open Area.

Window 2 is our Blind Area. In our Blind Area is included those behaviors, mannerisms, attitudes that we are not aware of, but many others around us are. These might include habits we have that turn people off, or things that we do that people like in us but we aren't aware that they like them. For example, an instructor who didn't understand why his students were afraid of him learned that when he talked to them he put his hands on his hips, spoke loudly and had a confrontational stance. He thought he was simply listening to the student. These behaviors were in his Blind Area. When his interfering behaviors and demeanor were revealed to him by the beauty school owner, his Blind Area was exposed and he opened up, let it in and consciously corrected his mannerisms. He was self-actualizing by expanding his Open Area, and making his Blind Area smaller.

How do we expand our Open Area and make our Blind Area smaller? By asking for feedback from our instructor and teammates, our clients and our friends. And asking in a way in which we are genuinely interested in becoming the best person we can by being open to their observations.

Window 3 is where our Hidden Area is found. In our Hidden Area are all of those thoughts and emotions that are known to us, but hidden to others. These include our sensitivities, fears, guilts, pleasures, hidden agendas, intentions and secrets. Our Hidden Area weighs the heaviest on us because we are cautious and defensive that no one discovers them.

How do we expand our Open Area and make our Hidden Area smaller? By sharing those things that are appropriate to share with others. Stylists often find it helpful and even therapeutic to open up and discover that the world doesn't end.

Learning about the Hidden Area, Wendy finally opened up to her fellow teammates. "I wish I could color like you guys. I love being here but I feel intimidated by how good you guys are." Support immediately came her way. "I had no idea, Wendy. Personally, I think you are a great colorist," Lisa shares. Wendy expanded her open area into both her hidden area by sharing, and Lisa's comment opened up Wendy's blind area.

Window 4 is our Unknown Area. In our Unknown Area exist our unconscious feelings, and our unknown motivations that affect our behaviors. You will learn about our unconscious minds in a later chapter. For the practical purpose of expanding our Open Area, the Unknown Area is the one we can affect the least.

As we look through our Johari Window with a desire to grow by expanding our Open Areas, we ask for feedback from others to make our Blind Area smaller and open up to others to make our Hidden Areas smaller.

How else we can grow through openness?

_____

_____

How can you expand your Open Area and make your Blind and Hidden Areas smaller?

_____

_____

2. Growing by Choosing to Be Growth-Centered, Not Self-Centered

One huge Washington state salon made a major change in their color line. The change forced the stylists to learn a whole new system of calculation totally foreign to them. Fear arose in the salon, naturally, and the stylists' anxieties over making mistakes were heightened. Gerard, a stylist in his late thirties, broke the other stylists' resistance with his courageous thoughts. "Look, I know it's going to be rough at first. It's a whole new process. It'll be hard for you, and hard for me. But wasn't learning the first system hard before we mastered it? We could have given up before and we didn't. Let's plug onward, let it in, and give it a try. In a short time, we'll master this new system and then we'll have knowledge of both." Gerard helped his fellow stylists to open up and take a courageous step toward mastering more of their salon world. Growth-centered people are open to new ideas because of the promise of self-improvement.

What is the difference between being a self-centered person and a growth-centered professional like Gerard? Consider a list of the differences:

> *Growth-centered people are open to new ideas because of the promise of self-improvement.*

Self-Centered Stylist	Growth-Centered Stylist
Fears making mistakes, looking bad, trying something new.	Loves the challenge of mastering new things.
Gives up after making a mistake.	Views mistakes as a very natural part of moving toward and mastering new things.
"Unless I'm perfect, I'm worthless. So I'll only do what I can do perfectly."	"I have the courage to be imperfect and take risks. When I make a mistake, I will simply correct it and learn from it."
When criticized by a client or manager, either insults their credibility or goes into a shell.	When criticized, thanks the client or manager for her input and thinks, "Because I'm not perfect, maybe there is something I can learn from the criticism to improve myself."
Resists new ideas and wants everything to remain the same.	Loves new experiences. Loves to improve and move toward mastery.
Wanders aimlessly throughout the day with no goals or very low goals.	Has specific, worthwhile goals, both long- and short-term.

Salons in the future will look different because the stylists in the salons will be different. They will be growth-oriented and have more of the "courage to be imperfect." They will see their fuller creative potential by growing when not being handcuffed to the fear of mistakes. They will also see the potential they have not just in the salon, but also in their lives.

Where in your life could you become more growth-centered? What is your plan?

_____

_____

3. Become a Criticism Welcomer

A self-centered thinker believes, "If I am criticized, it is a shot at my worth and I must immediately defend myself. I must continue to make excuses or find other people or things to blame to explain what happened. Or, if I must, I will start attacking my critic's shortcomings."

Contrarily, a growth-centered thinker concludes, "If I am criticized, I start with the fact that I am a fallible human who is in the process of becoming the best I can. So each day I look to improve and to become better and better. When someone suggests how I could have done something better, I appreciate him or her for taking the time to offer me ideas to improve. I take the criticism seriously and consider if I can use any of the ideas. If so, I change. The worst thing that can happen is that I can't make use of a suggestion. But either way, I thank the person who took the time to offer the suggestion."

That's a healthy, growthful approach to handling life's realities, isn't it? A growth- centered thinker is a criticism welcomer, a person who listens to criticism with the desire to improve and the ability to ignore insults.

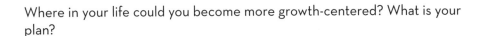

criticism welcomer, a person who listens to criticism with the desire to improve and the ability to ignore insults.

How Could You Handle Criticism to Help You Grow?

Think about the last time someone criticized you and you had a reaction. Through which lens did you use to view this criticism – your self-centered ego, or your desire to grow?

When you respond from your self-centered ego, you generate beliefs like "They're all wrong. Who do they think they are, telling me what to do? They aren't perfect. I can't stand it! I just hate them." And so on. You can predict the results of choosing to react from self- centered thoughts.

Now consider the same criticism. This time, develop goals generated by your desire to become a truly skilled Psy-Cosmetologist. Here is an example of a growth-centered reaction – "My goal is to become the best possible person I can be. I'll consider these ideas to see if I can use any of them to help me become a better person."

Keep in mind that the only people who have to be defensive are those who feel that their self-centered ego, their worth, is being attacked. The self-centered person is limited to this time, this place – and they are putting their total selves into defending a previous behavior. The growth-centered thinker is in-process, growing, improving with insights along the way, without experiencing criticism as an attack. Criticism is viewed as a form of mentoring. Free advice!

Yes, of course, there are mean people who launch attacks that are intended to hurt others. The growth-centered person has two reactions to this. First, the value of the criticism is not based on the person who gave it. Why would you not use the suggestions of a mean, angry dance teacher who hates you if the suggestions were valid and would help you become a better dancer? Secondly, if the mean, angry dance teacher who hates you gives you a destructive suggestion you can't use, then (and only then) the growth suggestion has no value for you.

How a Growth-Centered Psy-Cosmetologist Handles Defeats in Competition

Interestingly, another way in which a self-centered thinker fools herself and differs from a growth-centered thinker is in their view of the competition. A self-centered thinker believes, "If the competition beats me, I must put my opponent down and show I lost because of luck, cheating, dirty plays, or bad judging."

The growth-centered thinker concludes, "I was defeated today. I lost. So I'll congratulate my opponent, analyze the defeat, and make the necessary corrections that will increase the likelihood that I will achieve victory the next time. With this new information, and a good attitude, I'll be back and stronger than ever."

Who will grow more from the experience? The growth-centered stylist, of course. Who will be stuck? The self-centered stylist. Who will become greater from the same experience? Experience the important distinction between being self-centered and being growth-centered.

A Classy Reaction to a Setback

The style of a true growth-thinker is clearly demonstrated in one of the most interesting stories I've ever heard. In a flight from South Bend to Chicago, I had the opportunity to sit by Mike Smith, President of the Sugar Bowl Football Classic. Being interested in the thinking styles of famous athletes, this seating assignment gave me a chance to learn more about the personalities of the best college football players in the world. So I asked the president of the pigskin attraction to share a little bit of his insights with me about the greatest football players he had met as they related to self- and growth-centered thinking in handling defeat. With a big smile, the southerner whose presence commanded respect said, "The truly great athletes are those who don't have to brag. They can accept losing and move on without looking for excuses or blaming circumstances."

He went on to say, "Let me share one of the most touching experience I ever had with that kind of athlete. Each year one of my responsibilities is presenting The Sugar Bowl Outstanding Player of the Game Award. A few years back, Tony Dorsett was misinformed that he had won the award. The coveted trophy would be his for life! It was my responsibility to break the news to him that someone else, in fact, had been chosen in the last few plays of the game. In the hectic pace, with international TV present and viewers anxiously awaiting the presentation, I informed Tony of the news."

Stop for a second and imagine being Tony Dorsett at that moment, with your hopes up, feeling the pride of having your achievement acknowledged throughout the world, the implications for future contracts, etc.

Mike Smith continued, "After I told Tony, he paused briefly and asked if he could stay and be one of the first people to congratulate the winner."

That's class. That's also healthy living – living that moves one forward and gains respect as a role model for how a growth-centered thinker handles a challenging circumstance. Picture the reaction of a self-centered thinker and imagine the self-produced pain experienced by a self-centered thinker when he handles a defeat – stuck, living and re- living the decision of the judges.

Elevate Your Competition: It'll Reveal Your Confidence

As a psychotherapist, I would share stories and examples with my patients to help them understand the different ways self-centered and growth-centered people handle competition. And when they really understand the distinction between the two, it has the power to dramatically change their lives.

I recall a disheveled but attractive hairdresser whom I'll call Phyllis, hurting because her boyfriend was seeing another girl. Phyllis whined, "And I keep telling Tim how ugly she is and that she has nothing going for her. I just can't understand what he sees in her!"

"That's interesting, Phyllis. I mean, you say you're telling Tim how ugly the other girl he's seeing is? Wow! It strikes me that it would be much wiser to do just the opposite. I'd pick out all of her positive points and tell him about all of the great things she has going for her."

Startled, Phyllis looked at me in consternation and exclaimed, "Are you losing your mind? You want me to tell Tim about her positive points? Why should I do something as stupid as that?"

"Simple," I responded. "There are at least two major ways to beat your competition. The petty way, and in the long haul the most ineffective way, is to win by trying to put down your competition. But just think about how you view people who are always putting other people down. Do they look classy?"

After a few pensive moments, Phyllis responded, "Well, I, uh, I guess I sort of lose respect for them. I don't enjoy being around them. I'd rather be with somebody positi...." The young woman stopped mid-sentence. After a bit, she continued, "Maybe I'm losing Tim because I'm always putting her down. Perhaps I'm sickening to be around. But, if I'm positive and let Tim know about her good points, won't he just become more attracted to her?"

"Well, that too is up to you," I said. "Remember, Phyllis, I suggested that there are at least two possible ways of beating your competition. The first way is to put your opponent down. This is what we call a self-centered style. The second way to win is to pick up yourself. Start by praising the good points of your competition. This, in itself, picks you up because it shows people that you have so much confidence that you don't have to be a small thinker, even about your competition. Next, you pick up yourself by becoming a growth-centered thinker."

I continued, "You tell me that your goal is to win Tim over, right? So take all of the effort that you now use to put down his new girlfriend and re-direct it to become a new, exciting, even more beautiful person, both inside and out, who is positive and fun to be with all of the time. Let's look at all of the things you could do to achieve your goal. First, you could wear your hair a different way each time you're with Tim. Spend a little more time smiling. Start thinking about Tim's life and his interests, listen to what's going on in his world, and understand what he is proud of and excited about."

I stopped, waiting for Phyllis to reflect a little more on a growth-centering approach. Then I concluded our session by asking her, "So, Phyllis, it's up to you. You decide which would be more gratifying to you – losing to someone you feel is horrible or winning over competition who you feel is fantastic?"

To review, in dealing with the realities of life challenges, remember that the universe opens up new ideas to you when you are open to new ideas.

1. Become a criticism welcomer. When criticized, ask yourself how you can use the ideas to become a better person. Thank the critic for taking the interest and the time to help you grow.

2. Become a credit giver, not a credit taker

3. Make your growth more important than your pride.

4. Make defeat sweet by avoiding blaming, complaining, and excusing. Simply analyze how you can improve to become a better person.

5. Elevate your competition. Become a big, not a pint-sized, thinker.

Think of a time in your past when you were criticize and didn't handle it well.

What could you do to deal with the same criticism in a more growth-centered way?

_____

_____

4. Rise above Comparison Thinking

Avoid the trap of basing your value of yourself by making evaluations in relation to others. We call this comparison thinking. You have different experiences. You have a different gall bladder, heart, mind, and toenails – comparing yourself to any other person in the world is irrelevant to keeping you in the process of becoming all you can be. Consider the absurdity and small thinking of comparing yourself to others.

Imagine if we lined up every single person in the world according to his or her abundance in any dimension. Let's start with income. Imagine that all seven billion people were listed on a continuum in order from lowest to highest income. Where would you be on that list? Close to the top, we bet! Would you like to find out who was a step higher than you and what you needed to earn to rise on the list?

And what if you achieved that and started to get obsessed with this list? Could you possibly become so focused on this list that you would begin thinking day and night about how to overtake the next highest person and remain on attack alert, threatened by those just below you? When would you ever find anything but temporary happiness due to a shallow victory?

And what if you made the income list so important that you constantly dwelled on it? What would happen to you on the other lists – for example, your list about becoming a good father, mother, teacher, or friend? Could you possibly keep rising on both lists? What if we brought in other lists such as your physical, social, and spiritual health?

A Psy-Cosmetologist has a better way. Grow to be all you can be. If someone grows faster than you, congratulate her and take inspiration from her example by becoming better yourself. If you are going to compare yourself to anyone, compare yourself to your own possibilities.

Rise above the obsession of giving value to yourself in relation to the performance of others. Transcend comparison thinking. Become your best.

Who is a person you often compare yourself to? How could you convince yourself to "get over it?"

_____

_____

Tips to Be Open to Grow

1. Think of the last few times someone criticized you. Find one thing that you can take away from each of those criticisms that you can use to become a better person.

2. Explain the difference between being a self-centered ego-defensive thinker and becoming a growth-centered thinker.

3. Identify times in your life when you have observed self-centered thinking in people. When have you observed growth-centered thinking?

4. Find some examples in your life where you have used comparison thinking and valued yourself in relation to others.

5. Think of some healthier way of growing by using comparison thinking that a Psy-Cosmetologist might use, like comparing your current self to your best possible self.

If you've found these ideas meaningful, consider reading the book *Early Poppers: Secrets of Self-Starters* by Lewis Losoncy and Dennis McClellan.

For any questions, further dialogue, or challenges with material in this chapter, please email us at howardh@peoplemediainc.com.

Chapter 9
Highlight Your Strengths

You are alive! You choose your attitude. You can change a person's life through your work. You are open to grow. And, when you focus on your strengths, you realize you have a lot going for you.

People want to be around Psy-Cosmetologists. In addition to being lovers of life, with upbeat attitudes and open minds, they not only see the glass of water as half-full, they appreciate the beauty of the glass itself! These special salon artists have a laser-like **focus on strengths**. Psy-Cosmetologists center on what's good and right about themselves, others and life. That's why they are so refreshing to be around! For example, they have developed the ability to see what's right with a person's hair and talk about new looks that highlight it, rather than what's wrong and how they can attempt to hide it. They focus on the existing assets and potential in the client's hair, skin and nails. One beauty school instructor explained, "I mark the ones that are right, not the ones that are wrong. The student then corrects the ones that aren't marked and I mark them and soon the student has a perfect paper." Wow! Where was she when I was in first grade? Imagine a salon full of Psy-Cosmetologists noticing what's right with each other. Why can't that be a part of your salon culture?

What are some ways that you can highlight your strengths?

1. What's Good about You?

2. Be a Positive Person

3. Speak in the Positive Language

4. Highlight Your Efforts, Improvements and Contributions

1. What's Good about You?

One of the most important qualities for a person to have is a positive self-image. Our self-image is our view of ourselves. Our self-image can make us our own best friend or our own worst enemy. How important is our self-image? Maxwell Maltz, author of the bestseller *Psycho-Cybernetics*, wrote:

"When self-image change, everything in life changes. Researchers have shown that students have gone from "F" grades to "A" grades in a matter of weeks. Sales people have literally doubled their income, shy people have become respected leaders, and depressed people have developed a renewed enthusiasm for life through self-image changes."

Maltz continued, "The self-image is the key to the personality and human behavior. Change your self-image and you change your personality and behavior. But more than this.

The self-image sets the boundary of individual accomplishments. It defines what you can, and cannot be. Expand the self-image and you expand the area of the possible. The development of an adequate and realistic self-image will seem to imbue the individual with new capabilities, new ideas, and literally turn failure into success."

But what is our self-image? Imagine that a Webster Dictionary representative approaches you and says, "Webster would like to put you in our dictionary next year. Like all words in our dictionary that have definitions behind them, we'll need a definition in back of your name to define you. For example, one definition of the word pencil is "a rod-like shaped object filled with graphite or lead used for writing."

What would your definition be of yourself in six describing words. What are the first positive describing words that come to your mind? (eg. Happy, athletic, good stylist, etc.)

1)   3)   5)

2)   4)   6)

Now get a 3" x 5" index card. Put your name at the top of the card and list the six positive traits you listed above. This is your "STRENGTHS SHEET." In this chapter we are going to be adding positive words to help you create your new, more positive and motivating self-image.

What are some things that you have accomplished that gave you personal satisfaction?

1. In school:

2. In the salon:

3. At home (as a parent, husband, wife):

4. Challenges you overcame:

Include your thoughts on your accomplishments on your STRENGTHS SHEET. Who are the 3 people you respect most in the world? Name one thing you have in common with each.

1)

2)

3)

Add the names of the people you respect most and the trait you share with them to the STRENGTHS SHEET.

What is something in your life that you worked hard at and finally achieved? What qualities did it take in you to reach that goal?

1)

List this achievement on your STRENGTHS SHEET as well.

Now look over your STRENGTHS SHEET. You have a lot going for you, don't you? Feel free to add other strengthening thoughts as you go about your daily experiences and carry the sheet with you wherever you go to remind yourself of all your positive qualities.

2. Highlighting Yourself by Being a Positive Person

The world opens its doors for the upbeat, positive enthusiastic person. Start off every conversation with a high note. Be a good news giver. Find something positive to say to everyone you see, and always talk about what other people are interested in.

Here is a list of ideas on the different ways negative and positive people approach life.

Negative Person	Positive Person
1. Seeks advice from losers or people who will support a point of view that	1. Seeks out advice from winners, achievers, and UP people! Having

Negative Person	Positive Person
is down on life. Asks people who have either failed or haven't tried to achieve a task if the task is possible. They say, "No, don't waste your time. The down person gives up, sees successful people achieve the task, and claims they got lucky.	achieved these accomplishments themselves, they give the advice, "Sure, you can do it." The upbeat person is inspired, and this energy and motivation spur him onward to "find a way." In some cases, the positively motivated person will take a trip to spend a few moments with someone who is a top achiever in his field of interest, will attend lectures given by winners, will find consultants who are believers in overcoming the impossible, and will read books by people who overcame barriers and reached the top.
Finds excuses, looks for things or people to blame for being held back. "Why wasn't I born into money?"	Sees excuses for what they are – using energies to build a case for why one couldn't do it – instead of using energies to DO IT.
	When told by someone that you can't really get ahead if you're not born into money, explain, "Since 1928, only a few presidents of the United States were born into money, and that's one of the most powerful positions in the world."
Arrives at work down, drags everyone else down, feels persecuted by life.	Is a stimulant, a lifter to everyone at work. Everyone loves to be around this positive energy force who is missed when not in the salon.
Every day is the same. Same clothing, same haircut, same ideas on life. Dull, boring, negative.	Fresh, exciting, and creative. Brings new looks and new ideas, is stimulating and unpredictable. Takes a boring job and makes a game of it. Sends cards or writes letters to other people even when there isn't a birthday or any other event.

Negative Person	Positive Person
Takes credit for everything.	Gives credit to everyone; never takes credit.
Sees others in the salon as competition.	Sees other on the salon team as equals; cooperates and encourages others. Is a positive and constructive force in the salon environment.
Backbiter; always eager to talk about people behind their backs.	Is always up-front with people. If necessary can be assertive and deal with issues. Turns gossipy, backbiting conversations into productive ones. This person is, over the long haul, the most trusted friend of everyone in the salon.
Makes it unfashionable for others to say they actually enjoy hairstyling. Puts those who do down as "weird."	Proud to be part of the hairstyling profession and builds pride in others, especially those who go the extra mile for the client or the other professionals in the salon.
Gives orders to everyone.	Gives life and energy to others.
Sees what's wrong with everything, but doesn't attempt to change anything.	Sees what's right in others. Always starts off conversations with a compliment.
Sees problems.	Sees challenges and solutions.
Has to be constantly told what to do; not a self-starter. Has to be forced to attend educational shows or in-salon programs.	Self-igniting, responsible, anticipates problems ahead of time and has a plan to prevent things from getting worse. Seeks out educational programs; takes pride in learning new styles, textures, and colors.
Late; holds an irresponsible attitude toward professional responsibilities.	Ethical; understands professional responsibilities to clients, coworkers, and the salon.
Sees only one point of view (their own) and doesn't believe in the importance of a team- powered salon feeling.	Considerate of others and always tries to see the other side of the story in a disagreement. Salon professionals often turn to this person for help in solving conflicts between people.

Positive people are stimulants, magnets who attract others around them. The responsible, positive salon professional experiences many social, financial, physical, spiritual, and personal benefits that the negative person doesn't. Being positive isn't the result of being born in the right home or of getting the breaks in life. It is a personal choice.

Which of these positive ideas do you like the most and feel you can use? How will you use it to be more positive?

_____

_____

3. Speak in the Positive Language

Your words form your realities. Your words trigger your emotions. Watch what you say when you are talking to yourself, because you may be listening. Think of speaking to yourself in an uplifting manner as learning a new language – the Positive Language! When someone asks me how many languages I know, I respond, "Fluently? Two – English and Positive!"

Here are some samples of the Positive Language in action.

"Down" Words
I was "rejected" I "failed"
I "hate" It's "terrible"
I was "intimidated"
I am "overwhelmed"

"Up" Words
I was "misunderstood"
I'm "learning"
I "don't prefer"
It's "different"
I was "challenged"
I am "stimulated"

"Good" Words
I'm "alright"
I look "attractive"
I am "determined"
I am "energized"
I feel "great"
I am "okay"

"Great" Words
I'm "super"
I look "gorgeous"
I am "unstoppable"
I am "turbo-charged"
I feel "phenomenal"
I'm "fantastic"

Speaks with a "Down" Vocabulary
"Things are awful."

"I'm too old to change."

Speaks with an "Up" Vocabulary
"We face an exciting challenge here in the salon."
"My experiences give me an opportunity to change. The world is changing; my profession is changing. To stay in tune, I will not only change, but will enjoy the excitement of it."

Speaks with a "Down" Vocabulary	**Speaks with an "Up" Vocabulary**
"I'm too young to do that."	"Achievement doesn't discriminate against youth. Anyway, the biggest and most important part of trying something new is not in the achievement but in the learning one gets from the attempt. In my youth I can explore new things and can learn each time."
"Maybe it can be done."	"It absolutely can be done – and we here in the salon are made of the stuff that can do it. Let's get started."

4. Highlight Your Efforts, Improvements and Contributions

Where Are You Improving?

Psy-Cosmetologists have a mindset that values constant improvement. This helps them feel the rewards of progressing as they develop their skill. Myrna, a Pennsylvania stylist, explains it, "The first time you try something new, you don't do it perfectly. If you don't give up or get down on yourself, you'll see yourself improving. And then, one day, you'll finish a cut and see a nice clean line that demonstrates that the weight was properly placed. Never happens the first time."

When you think about it, the most we can do in life is to give our best efforts. We can't do more than that. Imagine trying to walk for the first time, falling, and concluding, "I tried walking once but I just can't do it. So I'll crawl for the rest of my life." Absurd, isn't it?

Think of all the things you can do today that you couldn't do when you were ten years old. Look at all the skills you acquired in beauty school that allowed you to become a hair, skin or nail professional. Isn't it reasonable to assume that there will be things you can't do today that you will be able to do tomorrow, or a year from now?

Remember this – if you don't make an effort, you won't be any better tomorrow than today. If you make an effort, you will grow and improve. You can never fail when you make an effort, because you will learn and improve with each attempt.

Always remember that growing is more important than succeeding. There are no limits to your future if you are going beyond your comfort zone and growing, improving and progressing through your efforts.

How Are You Contributing to Making a Better World?

How is the world a better place because of you? Think about how each of your client's lives are enriched because of you.

Consider how you are contributing to making your teammate's lives a little better, maybe a little lighter, maybe funnier or even happier.

How is your salon a better place because of you?

How is your family improved or helped by your presence?

In what ways have you helped your church, the clubs you belong to or the teams you have been on?

You made the difference!

Tips to Highlight Your Strengths

1. Focus on what's right with you, what's good about you and what strengths, assets and resources you have. Start building your STRENGTHS SHEET. Read it every day and keep adding to it.

2. Be determined to be a positive person today who lifts everyone you meet.

3. Speak in the Positive Language.

4. Reward yourself when you improve, not just when you succeed. What will you improve in yourself today?

5. Learn at least one new thing every day. What is something that interests you or something that could benefit you to know? Find out about it!

6. Focus on the ways you are contributing to a making a better world. How could you improve the world a little bit today?

If you've found these ideas meaningful, consider reading the book *Authentic Happiness* by Martin E. P. Seligman.

For any questions, further dialogue, or challenges with material in this chapter, please email us at howardh@peoplemediainc.com.

Chapter 10
Get Over Stuff Quickly

You are alive! You can create a winning attitude for yourself. You can change someone's life. Anything is possible if you open yourself up to grow. You have so much going for you. And if you have fun with the everyday inconveniences of life, you'll eventually find it easier to laugh than cry when problems arise!

Life is rarely perfect for us. In life, particularly when one is taking chances to better their life, setbacks will occur. If one is realistic, however, tons of frustration can be avoided!

How does one deal with tough challenges, like when Nioka Udvardy's Kalamazoo, Michigan salon was leveled by a fire? Her team-powered staff at Modern 3 Salon & Spa viewed the experience as a mere inconvenience, and were determined to rebuild their salon, making it bigger and better. Psy-Cosmetologists, like Nikki and her team, have the innate sense to immediately accept anything they can't change. They wasted little time getting themselves discouraged with the difficulties of life. If you ever need a little inspiration on how to get over stuff, check out Modern 3 Salon & Spa. It's bigger and better than ever!

Psy-Cosmetologist Shannon Bock of Sheldon, Iowa, remembers the Serenity Prayer when faced with struggles. "God grant me the serenity to accept the things I cannot change. That's the big one," she says with a smile. Shannon is known in Sheldon for her charity efforts, and can always offer a genuine word of encouragement to those in need of a lift.

In addition to acceptance, many Psy-Cosmetologists employ humor to help them deal with unfortunate events in their lives. They learn to laugh out loud at life. "Somebody like ME shouldn't have to get a parking space so far away from the salon," one Psy-Cosmetologist asserts, laughing at the ridiculousness of her statement. The realists don't take life personally and realize that there is no reason why life should be any easier on them than it is on everyone else.

What are some strategies Psy-Cosmetologists use to get over stuff?

1. Immediately Accept Anything You Can't (or Won't) Change

2. Use Your Perceptual Alternatives

3. Get Over Stuff through Humor

4. View Tough Experiences as Mere Inconveniences

1. Immediately Accept Anything You Can't (or Won't) Change

When our daughter was about four, she received a balloon from a TGI Friday's restaurant. She was so excited that when she got outside, her hands accidentally opened up and soon the balloon was up, up and away! The little one sat on the curb, crying out, "Daddy, I want that balloon. Bring it back."

As I sat beside her, I offered her a lesson about life and acceptance.

"Honey, we can go inside the restaurant and get you another balloon and it can be any color you want. If you need that particular balloon, however, we are going to have a real problem."

Fortunately for all of us, she was happy with the resolution of getting another balloon. This time she held to the string tightly and went home a happy girl. She learned the important lesson of "what is, is!" at an early age.

In thirty years of presenting psychology to salon professionals, there is one part of our program that they never forget. That is when I ask them to shout, "What is, is!" Shouting out these three words when facing a setback can save you hours of frustration, anger and all sorts of pain.

Do you remember from a previous chapter that we are not affected by what happens to us, but rather by the way we look at what happens to us? Telling ourselves "What is, is" reminds us that setbacks don't upset us, but what gets us crazy is what we keep telling ourselves about the setback. We can take the sting out of the negative event by simply shouting to ourselves, "What is, is!"

Try it. You won't believe how therapeutic these three words can be.

Just as acceptance is mentioned first in the Serenity Prayer, it is the first step to dealing with frustration and stress. But how do we accept the things we can't change? For a few suggestions on this matter we turn to a group of thinkers from over two millennia ago called the Stoics. Stoicism is a philosophy of life that values acceptance and resignation in the face of life's challenges. In my opinion, the best book ever written on the subject of the Stoics is William B. Irvine's *A Guide to The Good Life: The Ancient Art of Stoic Joy*. Irvine encourages the reader to think about all experiences and dilemmas by dividing them into three categories.

The Trichotomy of Control

Categories of Things	Example	The Stoics' Advice
Things over which we have complete control	The goals we set for ourselves, the values we form	We should concern ourselves with these things
Things over which we have no control at all	Whether the sun will rise tomorrow	We should not concern ourselves with these things

Categories of Things	Example	The Stoics' Advice
Things over which we have some but not complete control	Whether our client will be satisfied with the look we give her	We should concern ourselves with these things, but we should be careful to internalize the goals we form with respect to them.

By internalizing the goals, Dr. Irvine means that we focus on being our best and doing our best. We control that. We do not totally control the client's reactions to our work, so we should instead focus on honing our technical skill and broadening our knowledge of different cuts and procedures. More often than not, by centering on what we can influence we will perform better enhancing the chances of our client's satisfaction.

All right, let's practice. Mark each of these experiences as being something over which you have total control (TC), partial control (PC), or no control (NC).

Experience	Category
1) It's raining and you wanted to go to a picnic	1)
2) Winning a styling competition	2)
3) Setting goals each day in the salon	3)
4) Greeting every client with a smile	4)
5) Offering your clients a consultation	5)
6) A red light	6)
7) Being on time in the morning	7)
8) Not getting upset about a challenging client	8)
9) Re-booking a client	9)
10) Offering a client a rebooking	10)

Remember, immediately accept anything you can't or aren't going to change by shouting to yourself "what is, is!" For example, accept that you aren't going on a picnic outside in the rain – that is an NC event. Turn your energies to a TC event, like setting your next day's goals in the salon. If you set internalized goals over the things you have partial control (PC), like preparing to perform your best in your next styling competition, you will improve your chances of winning (although the judges have the final say).

2. Use Your Perceptual Alternatives

What is, is! The rules of reality are set forth by life, not by us. These rules continue to exist regardless of our personal feelings toward them. However, the good news is that we have full control of our own personal view of reality. And it is this – our own personal viewpoint of the world – that ultimately affects us.

Change in our life can occur on many levels. We can change the way we look at life (perceptual change) or the way we act in life (behavioral change).

The more ways we have of looking at life, the more capable we are of living fully by creatively adjusting to life. Discouraged people have a tendency to view life in a rigid, stereotypical, black-and-white fashion. They tend to react the same way to situations without generating creative and workable perceptions. Everything seems to be cut-and-dry to discouraged people. This keeps them restricted and limits their choices and experiences.

You can develop your skills in coping with life to reach your goals by developing your perceptual alternatives. In *Turning People On*, I introduced the concept of perceptual alternatives. Perceptual alternatives are the many different ways we have of viewing and interpreting any given situation.

> *Perceptual alternatives are the many different ways we have of viewing and interpreting any given situation.*

You are a bundle of complex and creative talents. In any given situation, you possess the ability to size up a situation and perceive it in many ways if you choose. From the many perceptions you generate, you can choose the most effective, realistic perception.

Try this perceptual alternative exercise with an object (pencil, paper clip, etc.) currently available for you:

Stand above the object and study it. Now look at it from the sides and concentrate. Pick it up, if possible. Consider the different ways of viewing the object. How is the object different according to the ways you look at it? How would the person who built this object view it? What is it made of? What are all of the different uses you could creatively make for this object? Do this for one minute, allowing your mind unlimited freedom. Jot down your responses:

_____

_____

Imagine! If you could find this many ways of viewing this one object in one minute, think about how many ways you have of viewing yourself, your complexity, and any circumstances or events in your life!

If you feel a sense of empowerment, you are developing perceptual alternatives, and even more importantly, you are on the road to greater self-encouragement. And, again, we ask you – is there a greater gift you can give yourself than courage?

Proof of Our Perceptual Alternatives

There have been many inspiring human experiences demonstrating the importance of perceptual alternatives.

Victor Frankl in *Man's Search for Meaning* wrote about his experience of being imprisoned in a war camp with little chance for survival. He described how the guards stripped him, starved him, dehumanized him. He said that the prison guards could treat him any way they chose (external reality), but the one thing they couldn't do was affect the way he chose to view his existence (perceptual alternatives).

Epictetus, the Stoic philosopher, wrote: "Disease is an impediment to the body [external reality], but not to the mind unless the will chooses it [perceptual alternatives]."

William Glasser, the founder of Reality Therapy, discussed alternatives in *Current Psychotherapies* when he wrote:

"Even a man facing a firing squad has some limited alternatives. He might pray, curse, collapse, spit, hold his breath, scream, try to escape to the best of his ability, face the firing squad with equanimity, bite his lip, stick out his tongue, and so on."

Rollo May, a psychoanalyst, commented on an interview with a patient on death row. Discussing his time in prison, the patient said, "A man can live without liberty [his prison experience – external reality], but he cannot live without freedom of will [perceptual alternatives]."

These writings are examples of how perceptual alternatives can improve the quality of your one life on the globe. If some of these individuals facing extreme stress could generate courage through, first, facing their real situation ("What is, is!") and, second, developing the most productive perceptual alternative for viewing their situation, imagine what we can do in our everyday life! Must we be confronted with our own death to appreciate the beauty of our life?

I believe that once you have developed your perceptual alternatives to view life's events, you are then in a better position to deal with these events. I suggest that perceptual alternatives show the potential path to both acceptance and self-actualization. Responsible human beings then choose the best behavioral alternative from their many perceptual alternatives.

3. Get Over Stuff through Humor

The universe doesn't revolve around you or me, does it? All of us experience times in our lives when we consciously or subconsciously believe the events in the universe are arranged around us personally. Psy-Cosmetologists have a clearer awareness of cause-effect relationships between self and the world, and don't take life events personally. Here are a few things Psy-Cosmetologists keep in mind:

- You missed your flight because of heavy traffic. That part is true. But the heavy traffic was not there for the purpose of keeping you from making your flight, was it?

- Do not take red lights personally. The reason you got ten red lights in a row is not that the lights varied their timing pattern because you were on the road. Their pattern would be the same whether you were there or not.

- An elevator does not stop on every floor just to get you bent out of shape because the elevator knows you have to get to a restroom immediately.

- Lines in the bank do not get longer immediately before you arrive to frustrate you personally. If you study the people in the lines closely, you will observe that they have more important things to do than tie up their time just to get you angry. You will notice that they are there to complete a transaction. And would you agree that they would have been there whether you were or not? You're not in the bank to frustrate someone else, are you?

- You have no greater chance of winning the lottery because you played your spouse's, your son's and your own birthday numbers, or playing any number at all. A few million others also played their family numbers and lost. And, did you not lose with those same numbers before as well? Anyway, how could it be that the machine that pulls up the table tennis balls with numbers on them made a decision to pick or not to pick your numbers?

- The TV remote should not be anywhere other than where it is. It should not be where you think you put it because it is not there. The remote has no legs and therefore is helplessly wherever it actually is.

- Your stock did not take a dive today because you invested in it yesterday.

- The weather does not want to make you miserable. It does not even know your name.

- The blackjack dealer at your local casino is not luckier than you. Well, perhaps you could say he is luckier, because he is making money and you are losing it. Plus, the odds are in his favor. Frankly, he is cheering for you to hit big – because then you will tip him for being your good luck charm!

- The state trooper did not let the person in front of you off the hook and signal you out because you were you. Did you ever see a person get a speeding ticket who was not speeding?

- Friends did not drop in just because they knew your place would be a mess. Do you plan your visits based on when you think your friend's place will look like a junkyard?
- Are you a little offended when someone asks what astrological sign you are and then explains who you are based on your birthday? What about the unique personal you?

Are you successful because you are a certain sign? If so, would we find that people who are born in the same second as you are identical in every dimension? Relax, the universe does not revolve around you personally.

Use your sense of humor and realize that something that gets you upset wasn't organized by the universe to personally attack you.

---

4. View Tough Experiences as Mere Inconveniences

Our words are biochemical triggers. The words we choose are powerful and affect our emotions and our actions in life. The stoics tell us that there is a reality "out there" that is part of a cosmic nature that "is there." What is, is! But the tool we have to deal with the challenges "out there" is the way we look at them and the words we choose to use to frame them.

For example, when we view an event as devastating, awful, horrible, or as a catastrophe, at that very moment we are sending signals to our body to go into a panic mode. We can take the sting out of an event by viewing the event more rationally – by seeing it as a mere inconvenience.

My friend Dan Austin is a well-known Columbus, Ohio resident who is a leading expert in skin care. Some years ago, while traveling though Russia, a major crisis erupted in which the Russian president Boris Yeltsin was kidnapped. Chaos was present throughout the country, especially in Moscow. At one point, a tank came up some steps in a face-off with Dan and his group. Dan later told me that as the other members of the group panicked, he reassured them by letting them know this was just an inconvenience. People who were in that group still talk about Dan's healthy view three decades later! The worst you'll ever experience is an inconvenience.

Years ago, I was speaking to a group of hairdressers in Des Moines, Iowa. I had just mentioned to the audience that "that most you'll ever experience in life is an inconvenience," when I tripped over a microphone wire and fell off the stage. The polite Midwesterners were all very concerned. I picked myself up, walked back onto the stage, looked at the group, and concluded, "Well, that is an inconvenience because I fell and hurt myself. It, however, is not a tragedy because I choose not to label it a tragedy. It could have been, but I don't have time for a tragedy today."

Hearing the laughter, I then asked if they thought I should have fallen. And then I gave them the answer: "Of course I should have fallen because the only thing underneath my feet was air and gravity was in operation today, as in all days here on Earth."

Years later, a member of that audience accidentally drove her car into her own beauty salon. Her husband was in the car with her. She was in a state of panic. Then her husband asked her, "What would Dr. Lew say about this situation?" She told me later that amidst her panic, she thought about it, looked at all of the damage, and replied, "He would say that this is just an inconvenience." She broke into a smile, there in those challenging circumstances, by taking the sting out with a stoic view that added humor and lightened up a real challenge. It certainly was an inconvenience because her salon had to be rebuilt. But when it was rebuilt, better than ever, she was so proud, telling me, "I couldn't have done this if it was a tragedy.

But I could do it because it was just an unfortunate inconvenience."

The most anything can be is an inconvenience – or maybe even an annoyance!

Talk Sense to Yourself

2,400 years ago, the Stoic philosophers fervently believed that the way we look at life has an impact on our experiences. Our words play a huge role in how we frame our reality. The words we choose become triggers for selecting one emotion over another. Salespeople, for example, are quite aware of how important it is to use the right words at the right time to influence buying behavior. Consider how the use of the words can alter emotional reactions. Look at the way a meal is described on a menu:

Open faced, hickory-smoked steak sandwich garnished with mushrooms in a

Bordelaise sauce and complemented with pommes frites made from Idaho's finest potatoes... $19.50

The meal was delivered. It was a chopped steak sandwich with French fries! For $19.50?

Here is a list of eight suggestions to change your language from discouraging to encouraging:

1. Go from passive, irresponsible **to** Active, responsible
"You made me..."   "I chose to..."
"The world made me..."   "I made myself..."

2. Go from "I can't"   **to** "I won't"
"I can't assert myself to my boss." "I won't assert myself to him."
             "I'm choosing not to..."

3. "If only... then I could" **to** "It would have been better if..."
"If only my mom had... then   "It would have been better if my mom had
I could be a success."   encouraged me."

4. Shoulds, oughts and musts **to** "I would prefer if..."
"It shouldn't rain this much."   "I would prefer it if it didn't..."

5. Exaggerating language   **to** Rational, factual language
"I fell while dancing. It was   "I fell while dancing, so I picked myself up
horrible. I was devastated!"   and started dancing again!"

6. Negative expectations   **to** Positive expectations
"I'll try, but I'll never do it."   "I'm going to get this done."

7. They say...   **to** Who says? Where's the proof?
"They say I should eat   "Who says? Why? I don't even like spinach."
spinach."

8. Generalizing language   **to** Specific, factual language
"I could never..."   "In the past I wasn't able to... but I've noticed
   that each time I do this, I get better.

What current challenges are you facing? Begin viewing them as inconveniences and see how your outlook changes.

Tips to Get over Stuff Quickly

1. If there are things you need to accept, wash your hands of them, shout, "What is, is," and move on.

2. Once you accept that you aren't going to change a situation, evaluate your perceptual alternatives to change your outlook and focus your energies on other challenges.

3. Sense when you are taking an event on the Earth personally and find the humor in it.

4. When you get upset or face a crisis, remember – it's just an inconvenience.

If you've found these ideas meaningful, consider reading the book *A Guide to the Good Life: The Ancient Art of Stoic Joy* by William B. Irvine.

For any questions, further dialogue, or challenges with material in this chapter, please email us at howardh@peoplemediainc.com.

Chapter 11
Find A Way

SHARON WOULDN'T BE
INTERESTED IN ANYTHING
BUT A CUT...

SHARON WANTS TO LOOK
THE BEST SHE CAN.
I HAVE A NEW HIGHLIGHTING IDEA
FOR HER THAT SHE'S GOING TO LOVE!

You are alive! Need we say more? Yes, you choose your attitude, and are self-motivated. You can turn someone's day around, are open to grow, and have so many positive things going for you. You are accepting the things you can't change, and now you are taking the motivating view that your challenges have solutions. Life is good!

A salon full of Psy-Cosmetologists is different in one important way. Every team member is optimistic and proceeds as if all challenges have solutions somewhere in their collective, creative human minds. "Believe you can or believe you can't and either way you'll be right," Henry Ford observed.

New Jersey salon manager Gina explains, "When we set new goals, we all act as if we can find ways to reach them. We don't doubt it for a minute. And we start brainstorming every possible idea, and soon, we have a plan! We got it! Imagine if, up front, we would have concluded that the ideas wouldn't work because of the economy, or because of our neighborhood, or because we are understaffed. Pessimism and doubting don't work too well."

You go Gina! Isn't Gina onto something? Can't never could!

What are some ways Psy-Cosmetologists make things happen?

1. Believe Challenges Have Solutions

2. Build a Lifting Environment To Keep You Up!

3. Tap the Power of Your Subconscious Mind

5. Get Things Done NOW!

1. Believe Challenges Have Solutions

The 17th Century philosopher Baruch Spinoza concluded that for as long as you believe something is impossible, you will notice that for that exact period of time it will be impossible. The very moment you see a dream as reachable that is the very moment you will go on to conquer that dream. Every great achievement was accomplished because of someone who knew that it could be done. The placing of the flag on the moon, the hair color you use, the idea of shears and all of your professional tools all started out in the hearts and heads of individuals who were much like yourself.

Please memorize these precious thoughts from the great psychologist, William James. After all you are a Psy-Cosmetologist who is learning from the great thinkers of motivation. James wrote:

"Sow a thought, reap an action,
Sow that action, reap a habit,
Sow that habit, reap a character,
Sow that character, reap a destiny!"

Your thoughts are things. One of your thoughts is to believe you can do it. Or if you choose to believe that you can't do it, just imagine how different your feelings, your motivation and your actions will be! Isn't it true that every success story was a story of a person who chose belief and determination, rather than doubt and retreat? Success involves changing these thoughts from being an average thinker to thinking how a Find-A-Wayer Psy-Cosmetologist thinks?

Average Stylist Thinker	Psy-Cosmetologist Thinker
"Sharon wouldn't be interested in anything but a cut."	"Sharon wants to look the best she can. I have a new highlighting idea for her that she's going to love!"

Just imagine how choosing the Psy-Cosmetologist's thought will advance your thoughts, feelings, motivation, and success! And then, on top of all of that, the most important benefit – seeing the response of your client who wants to look the best that she possibly can. And you'll have believed in her.

When would be a good time to bring out your optimism by proceeding as if the solution to a challenge is somewhere in your creative mind?

_____

_____

2. Build a Lifting Environment To Keep You Up!

Congratulations! We have good news for you! You have just been selected for one of the most prestigious positions in your world. We are pleased to announce that today, you begin your new post as Director of Environmental Engineering for the most important account in the world – your own.

Just as the air you breathe in your physical environment affects your physical health, your psychological environment affects your psychological health. When pollution levels are high, the contamination you breathe in circulates throughout your body. When the negative thought pollution in your environment is high, it is difficult for you to be a creative, enthusiastic, goal-directed person.

Take charge today. Engineer a massive cleanup of your attitude environment by eliminating polluted thinking. Create a fresh, idea-inspiring Spring-morning-feeling in your surroundings. Then watch your creative ideas, powered by your enthusiasm, flow into successful actions.

Your Environment Is Also a Product of You

Your environment is a powerful influence on you. In fact, the most popular school of psychological thought in the 1960s was Behavioral Psychology, largely credited to the brilliant B.F. Skinner. Behaviorists, as the advocates of Skinner's view were called, argue that people are a product of their environment. Skinner believed that we could understand all we know about people simply by understanding their environments. To change behavior, the behavioral engineer would simply alter the environment. That meant to reward or reinforce a person's behavior every time they did something positive. The person would then change as a result.

An environment with an abundance of reinforcers tends to invite positive behavior, whereas a negative environment tends to invite discouragement. While environment is important, a person is not totally and helplessly a product of his or her environment. In fact, the opposite is even true; that is, your environment is also a product of you. This powerful view asserts that you are an active creator of your environment rather than just a passive marionette dangling from the strings of the rewards given by people around you.

If you doubt that you play a role in creating your environment, try a simple test. The next time you go to a restaurant, give a warm smile to your waiter or waitress. Observe the reaction of your server to this positive approach. Now approach another server with a gruff "Where were you? I've been waiting a long time!" Contrast the two responses you receive and see if the environmental reactions differ when you change your style.

Yes, you are Director of Environmental Engineering for the construction of a positive setting for personal success. And the great news is that you have many, many people and unlimited natural resources to assist you in developing a winning environment. Your new environment can start and end on a positive note. Good luck in your new role!

Designing an Environment To Work For You:

1. Put positive people in your environment

2. Hire a board of positive consultants to help design your environment

3. Expose yourself to positive media

Put Positive People in Your Environment

Raise your ecological standards. No longer allow yourself to be a dumping site for rotten reasoning, noxious negativism, or poisonous perceptions. Stop feeding your thoughts on the failure fodder so plentiful in environmental dumping sites. Lower the motivation pollution index in your environment.

The first step in your environmental engineering cleanup is to surround yourself with the most positive people you know. When you do, you will become more creative, more enthusiastic, and more goal-centered, and you will even develop a more positive self-image.

Most negative people can be easily recognized and quickly diagnosed. Engineer out of your environment people who use opening lines like:

• "I shouldn't tell you what people are saying about you and your ideas, but..."

• "Let me play devil's advocate for a minute..."

• "You were never very good at..."

• "I wouldn't waste my time with that idea of yours..."

• "You! You could never..."

Also stay away from people who always have tragic, "doomsday" news or people who are worried about things like the sun running out of energy in the next seven billion years.

When people focus on the negatives in life or on your negative behaviors, they are trying to lead you down Loser's Lane to show you where they live.

"Hire" a Board of Positive Friends to Help You Make a Good Choice

Don't take on a challenge as important as designing your environment by yourself. As Director of Environmental Engineering, you have the power not only to de-hire but to hire people to assist you, Hire your own board of free advisors to be part of your successfully stimulating environment.

The simplest task in the world is selecting the people who will be on your board of positive consultants. Identify at least five people based on the following qualifications: (1) you feel positive about yourself and your life when you are with them, (2) you feel courageously willing to try new experiences and take new risks when you are with them, and (3) you feel free to speak and share even your craziest new ideas in their presence. Take this important exercise to heart.

Jot down the names of people you have honored as your selections. In your environment, a positive friend is like a rare gem.

1.

2.

3.

4.

5.

When you have identified the people you would like on your board of advisors, make a point of telling each person that you have read a book on the importance of having positive consultants. Tell each person the three requirements for being a positive advisor and that you have selected him or her for the position. Then ask each of your choices to consider accepting a position on your advisory board and express your confidence in the fact that acceptance involves nothing more than continuing to be himself or herself. Your comments will elate each of them. How would you feel if someone complimented you by saying that out of everyone he or she knew, you were one of the most positive influences on his or her life? After you share your news, you will find that these people are rarely "down" in your presence.

Become determined to spend more time with each of your board members in the future. Make plans to see them and talk with them, even if only on the telephone. When you consider the fact that people pay hundreds of dollars to talk with a psychiatrist or listen to a motivational lecturer, friends who help you feel positive are worth quite a lot. Don't neglect positive advisors, your richest source of input.

And the great news is that even if you can't be near your board of advisors because of distance or timing, it doesn't matter. When facing a difficult decision or a challenging situation, recall your advisors' thinking by visualizing their reactions to the event. In your imagination, recount the situation to each positive person and picture each one's response and advice. You will find that it is quite easy to picture what each board member might say. Most of your advisors would probably agree on the best course of action for you!

You also might add an honorary board of advisors made up of the most inspirational thinkers in the world. Why not?

Expose Yourself to Positive Media

Just as the air you breathe affects your health, negative media, whether it is television, radio, websites, or newspapers, affects your attitude. Wipe out the media pollution from your life. One of the easiest ways to get the wrong picture of life is to blindly accept all that you see in the media as truth. Sometimes a report or story can be very one-sided.

A few years ago, I was in a Midwestern city to speak at a high school graduation. On the way to the school, my cab driver asked what brought me to the Midwest. I explained that I was there to speak to the high school graduates about how to think their way to success. The cab driver put on his brakes and, peering through the rear-view mirror, sneered, "Teenagers and positive attitudes. Hah! I'll tell you about teenagers. Did you see the headline of today's paper?" He showed me the paper; the headline was something like "Two Boys Caught Starting Warehouse Fire." The cab driver added, "That's the kind of kids we have today."

Taken back by the cab driver's conclusion, I asked, "How many kids do you have in your city?" "Oh, about forty thousand," the cab driver said. I responded, "Forty thousand! Why, sir, if I were creating the headline for today's newspaper, the same story would have read, 'Rejoice! 39,998 of Our Children Not Caught Starting a Fire Last Night.' That's 99.99%. The headline reflected less than one-thousandth of the truth." The cab driver had treated the headline as though that's the way all kids are. Incredible!

I shared my experience in the cab with western Pennsylvania school superintendents and board members. One of the school superintendents, Dr. Leo Bourandas, from Butler, Pennsylvania, picked up on the idea, and a few weeks later sent me a copy of the Butler Eagle newspaper. The headline read, "School Superintendent Cites Good Kids." As I read the article, I was elated to see that in every category of discipline, more than 90% of the students had not violated the rules. Wouldn't you make the Butler Eagle your newspaper?

What can you change to make your attitude more upbeat?

_____

_____

3. Tap the Power of Your Subconscious Mind

Our conscious mind is our choosing and directing mind. When I tell myself, "I am going to go to the mall to get a sweater," I am making a conscious decision to drive to shop rather than to sleep or eat. But to whom am I mentally

> *Our conscious mind is our choosing and directing mind.*

speaking, since there is no other person in the room? Think about it. Who is my conscious mind talking to when I am mumbling to myself? In other words, my conscious directing mind is talking directly to my subconscious mind, my achieving, doing mind that follows the directions of the conscious mind.

> *subconscious mind, my achieving, doing mind that follows the directions of the conscious mind.*

Our conscious mind cannot do, or get things done. It can only choose **what to get done and whether or not it can be done**. Our subconscious mind cannot choose and direct, but it can use its unlimited creative files of resources to achieve the wishes and directions of our conscious directing mind. When the directing mind believes something can't be done, for example, telling ourselves that, "You could never earn that much money," then the subconscious mind finds ways to prove that it can't be done. Our subconscious minds follow the direction of our conscious minds and use its creativity to fulfill our conscious mind's beliefs.

If conscious telling, directing, and choosing mind says, "I CAN'T do it"	**BUT IF**	If conscious telling, directing, and choosing mind says, "I CAN do it"
THEN		**THEN**
Subconscious listening, following, doing and achieving mind will find reasons why you CAN'T do it (following conscious mind's direction):		Subconscious listening, following, doing and achieving mind will find reasons why you CAN do it (following conscious mind's direction):
"I'm not smart enough."		"First I'll learn everything I need to in order to be able to do it."
"It's too hard."		"I'll read books on the topic of what I'm trying to do."
"I'll just fail if I try."		"I'll practice every free minute."
		"I won't let not succeeding at first get in my way! I want to do this!"

Recently arriving home to our condo in Philadelphia, I forgot to push the elevator button to direct it to go to the 16th floor. Some others who live in the building had their numbers in place. So the elevator stopped at 4, then 11, then 12, passed 16 and headed to its final stop at 20. I was temporarily annoyed wondering why it didn't stop at 16. But my friendly neighbor from 20 reminded me that I didn't press 16. Just as I forgot to direct the elevator where to go, you could say that my conscious directing mind did not give my subconscious mind (the elevator in this analogy) a message as to what to achieve. In the absence of consciously telling our subconscious minds what to get done, with the optimistic message that "you can do it," then our subconscious, achieving mind resorts to habits or listens to the directions of others around us.

In *Science of Mind*, Dr. Frederick Bailes encourages the reader to think of our mind as the ocean. There is the surface, the see-able part of the ocean. This is by far the smallest part, and is like our conscious mind that is aware. Our subconscious mind is what is under the surface like the deeper part of the ocean, which extends six, eight, ten miles down. Our subconscious mind is our vast library of experiences, even genetic experiences from the history of humankind. Our subconscious mind can use its resources to find a way how we can or can't achieve something based on the directions of our conscious mind. Imagine all of these resources we have for success. And imagine the different results the optimistic conscious mind gets from the pessimistic conscious mind.

Consider the various functions of both conscious and subconscious mind.

Surface Conscious, Directing Mind	Deeper Subconscious, Creating, Doing Mind
The seed	The soil
Makes all choices	Turns conscious mind's thoughts into things
	Manifests wishes of conscious mind
Believes or doubts	Finds evidence to support conscious mind's beliefs of whether something is possible or not
Learns a phone number	Memorizes number
	Habitual mind
	Maintainer of the body
	Storehouse of our experiences

When you think of conscious mind, you could also think of it as containing seeds. Subconscious mind contains the fertile soil to grow any seed. When conscious mind plants those apple seeds into subconscious mind soil, subconscious mind will follow the genetic code and grow the apple trees. Subconscious mind cannot turn an apple seed into a peach tree. And conscious mind doesn't have the soil to grow the apple tree. We need both our conscious, directing, believing mind and our deeper subconscious achieving mind to achieve success. Nothing is more devastating than having a conscious mind that doubts because than the vast resources of our subconscious mind is used to support the doubts and prove it can't be done.

Without directing the elevator to 16, my life is up to luck and chance. When I consciously push 16 I am headed to my goal of being home.

Dr. Bailes offers some cautions to avoid bringing out the worst of our subconscious minds.

1) Eliminate negative speech- remember when conscious mind tells subconscious mind "you can't possibly do this," subconscious mind will use of its power to find evidence to support the negative wishes

2) Never say something about yourself that you don't want real-ized

3) Direct your subconscious mind to start acting like the person who you are in the process of becoming

4) Turn away from past failures

5) Turn to past successes no matter how small

6) We tend to attract what we expect because our subconscious mind has its vast tentacles searching in the direction of the expectations of conscious mind

7) Whatever we focus on we give our power

4. Get Things Done NOW!

Procrastination is tougher than facing the challenge. If you've made it to third base in life, get it done and go home for the run. Your next goal is much easier to attain than you may think and is, in the long run, much more fulfilling than procrastination.

Charles, a stylist, is 20 pounds overweight, and he tells everyone at the salon that he is starting a diet. That evening, Charles is dining with a few other stylists, and to everyone's surprise he orders a five-course meal. While they look at Charles with disappointment, he explains that he has decided to start his diet the next morning. Consequently, the distance to his goal will be increased. The next morning his goal will have to be to lose 22 pounds instead of 20. Plus, he will be a day older. His illogical, irrational reasoning was that it would be just as easy for him to start tomorrow. But as can easily be observed, it will be just the opposite. Each day the task becomes progressively harder. Procrastination is tougher than facing the challenge NOW.

Every day, Dorothy, a salon manager, lives with anxiety, believing there is something gravely wrong with her health. She experiences every symptom in the medical books and every symptom of the diseases that she reads about in the weekly magazines. She continually complains to everyone about her problems but refuses to go to a doctor. "After the new year," "after Easter," "sometime following vacation" are her seasonal reasons for procrastinating. And each week so many more things build up and feel wrong that she convinces herself that nothing will help. She begins to believe that she is better off just sitting around waiting to die. Dorothy's failure to face the problem by going to her doctor causes her a daily problem of worry and anxiety that becomes almost unbearable. She fails to realize that if she finds what is wrong, it can be dealt with. She also fails to recognize that her worries can actually produce further problems. There even exists a good possibility that if she goes to a doctor, she would find the problem was just a small one. Procrastination is tougher in the long run than dealing with the problem head-on and immediately.

The GIST of Success: Get It Started Today

Be a GIST person. Get It Started Today. Every single success story tells of a "magic moment," an "aha!," or a determined "Now is the time to start." And every failure has numerous tales of "I could have..." or "If only..." or "Someday I will...." Just observe the people around you. Some are GIST people. They see a **problem, they set a goal, and they proceed to Get It Started Today.**

Overcoming Procrastination with GIST Action

What are the three major explanations or excuses used to justify waiting rather than acting? The successful GIST person can defeat any one of them. Identify your major excuse and combat it forever.

Excuse for Waiting

1. Assuming the identity of a helpless procrastinator. "I'm the kind of person who puts off things until they are overdue."

"I work better under pressure."

2. Wait until conditions change. "Someday I want to start an exercise program; maybe in the summer when I can run outside."

GIST Action

1. Absurd! Even if in your past you were always late, it is inaccurate to conclude that this is the way you will always be.
2. You will be the kind of person today that you choose to be today.
3. Say, "I'm the kind of person who gets things done immediately." Build that identity into yourself and Get It Started!
4. Remember, procrastination is tougher than facing the challenge!

1. If you want conditions to be right, you will probably wait forever, so get on with it today.
2. Starting today makes conditions right.
3. Join a club or spa or exercise at home.

Excuse for Waiting	**GIST Action**
	4. Consult an expert and write a program for yourself that is reasonable and realistic.
	5. Encourage some other friends to join in with you.
	6. Be determined to make exercise as much a part of your life as eating or sleeping.
	7. When discouraged, remember the GIST principle and act. Instead of focusing on the problems of getting there or the energies that you will have to expend, focus on the great feeling you will have when finished.
	8. Take pride in your self-discipline.
	9. Get It Started Today.
3. Fear of failure. "I'd probably fail if I tried, so I might as well not try."	1. True, life has no guarantees and every time a person tries something new, the person could fail, but. . .
	2. The simple fact is that unless you change something in your life, it is unlikely that your life will get any better.
	3. Should you fail, remember, never be intimidated by what you did, only by what you didn't do but could have done.
	4. Failure to act is the biggest failure of all. Imagine if you were in a car and decided to pass another car. While you were in the passing lane, you saw another car coming right at you. Failure to act by either going faster or going slower could lead to a catastrophe.
	5. Even if you do fail, you simply correct your mistakes.
	6. If you Get It Started Today, you will have more time and more chances to perfect your plan and ensure success.

What are you going to get started on NOW? What is your first step? When is your goal to have achieved it?

_____

_____

_____

_____

_____

Tips to Make Things Happen

1. Proceed as if your challenges have solutions. Success comes in "cans."

2. Consider challenges that are in front of you. Tell your subconscious mind there are solutions to these challenges.

3. Design an environment around you that will lift you and encourage you to improve.

4. Consult your "advisory board" whenever you face a challenge.

5. Get It Started Today! Remember, in the long run procrastinating is tougher than facing a challenge.

For any questions, further dialogue, or challenges with material in this chapter, please email us at howardh@peoplemediainc.com.

Part 3
PSY-COSMETOLOGISTS ARE PEOPLE-SENSITIVE
The Psy-Cosmetologist's 6 Person-Centered Skills

You, of course, are well aware of the importance of coloring, texturing, styling and other technical skills to be successful. After all, you're an expert in the field of cosmetology! However, stylists really retain clients if their technical skills are accompanied by great people skills.

In your new field of Psy-Cosmetology, you will be acquiring the most important human relations skills in these next six chapters.

First Impression Skills will help you to win people over at first contact, while helping them feel safe and comfortable with you.

By using your **Bonding Skills** you will find yourself building immediate connections with people and befriending them over time.

Empathizing Skills will get you in touch with your client's feelings and help them to feel you understand their desires.

Specializing Skills will help each of your clients to feel special and unique.

Your **Energizing Skills** will bring excitement, enthusiasm and energy into your relationship with your clients, while adding extra value to your professional products and services.

And your **Encouragement Skills** will give your clients the courage to "Go for it!"

Soon you will be mastering these six Psy-Cosmetology human relations skills. But first, take a few seconds to learn these laws of service sensitivity.

10 Laws of Service Sensitivity

What Our Clients Are Saying to Us

1. The more a client feels a stylist likes them, the more they will like the stylist. (Attraction-reciprocation effect.)

2. The more a client feels a stylist is similar to them, the more a client will feel they know the stylist. (Similarity-comfort effect.)

3. The more a stylist is consistent with the client, the more the client will trust you. (Consistency-trust effect.)

4. The more benefits a client feels a stylist has that they want, the more they will listen to what the stylist has to say. (Benefits-interest effect.)

5. The more a stylist listens to a client's unique needs, the more information a stylist will have about the client's likes and dislikes. (Understanding-needs satisfaction effect.)

6. The more a stylist customizes their approach to a client's likes and dislikes, the more a stylist's methods will catch the client's attention. (Uniqueness-attention effect.)

7. The more enthused a stylist is about a client's possibilities, the more the client will see new potential in themselves. (Enthusiasm-bigger goals effect.)

8. The more hair problems a stylist solves, the more loyalty a client will feel to them. (Problem resolution-loyalty effect.)

9. The more a client is encouraged to grow and try new things, the more the stylist-client relationship will remain fresh. (Encouragement-excitement effect)

10. The more important a client feels, the more successful a client will help a stylist become. (Important-reciprocation effect.)

Chapter 12
First Impression Skills: Greet People Warmly

Isn't it interesting that there are some people you meet and like immediately? What is it they did that pulled you in? They had "First Impression Skills." First impression skills involve giving off initial positive vibes to help your client feel welcomed and safe.

First impression skills involve giving off initial positive vibes to help your client feel welcomed and safe.

Everywhere you go, there are opportunities to learn about the long lasting power of first impressions. Study how you are greeted in restaurants, at the doctor's office, or by cab drivers, police, or even in the department of motor vehicles. Be determined to become an expert in how to offer a warm, welcoming invitation to people.

But first, why are first impressions so important?

The Power of First Impressions

Our first impression is the frame into which we fit everything we observe later. In one study, half a class of students were told that their guest instructor was considered a very warm person who was industrious, critical, practical and determined. The other half of the class was told their instructor had the same qualities except the first words they heard were not, "very warm person," but instead, "cold person." In other words, to this half of the class, he was said to be a cold person who was industrious, critical, practical and determined. After the lecturer spoke for 20 minutes the class rated their teacher. The students who expected him to be warm rated him much higher than those who were told initially he was cold. Yet they all had the same instructor! Their first impression lasted no matter what they were told or actually experienced later. This supports the popular phrase, "you never get a second chance to make a first impression."

Most people draw a conclusion about whether they like or dislike, whether they feel comfortable or threatened, and whether they trust or mistrust someone within 2-3 minutes. When a stylist offers a warm smile to the client when greeting them for an appointment, the client will begin to feel relaxed even before their shampoo.

Remember, first impressions can be made without a formal introduction. New salon clients and "walk-ins" are sometimes curious about which of the stylists will be doing their hair, and will scan the salon while in the waiting area. Without knowing it, all the stylists on the floor are giving off first impression vibes. If a particular stylist is performing impressively and has a visibly pleasant demeanor, a person coming in to make an appointment may even point them out and ask for their schedule! Or, at least, they are hoping, "I hope it's her who'll be doing my hair."

Our Senses Give Us Our Impressions

Our five senses, what we see, hear, feel, taste and smell, along with our "sixth sense," intuition, determine our impressions. So we make our first impression by connecting warmly to our new client's ears, eyes and touch. Perhaps we can even enhance their sense of smell in the salon environment, or even stimulate the taste sense with fresh coffee.

Let's consider each of these separately.

Warm Up Your First Touch

Shaking hands is a great start to giving a positive first impression. Your warm, safe touch symbolizes reaching out to the person, welcoming her into your salon. When extending your hand, you are not only communicating caring, but you are already learning about your new client. Those who have studied the psychology of handshakes offer a few suggestions.

1. Sense whether your client would feel more comfortable with you using one or two hands in your handshake. While some argue that two handed handshakes are a little aggressive at a first meeting, I believe that in the salon, where the client has chosen to be there, a two-handed handshake reveals caring and reassurance.

2. Avoid crunching the other person's hands. This is too aggressive.

3. Avoid a "wet fish" wimpy handshake because it may reveal lack of confidence in oneself.

4. Keep your hands facing side to side. If your hand is on top, it may suggest dominance. If your hand is on the bottom, it could give vibes of timidity.

Ideally, aim for moderate firmness, have palms sideways, neither on top or on the bottom, and have your hands be dry. People who offer a firm handshake were immediately judged to be "open to new experiences," and "outgoing." Those with a weak handshake were viewed as being "anxious" or "shy."

The advantage of the handshake is not only that you are communicating a warm welcoming, as well as revealing your confidence, but you are learning about your new client. If your client's hands are moist it might mean she is a little anxious and needs more reassurance to feel secure with you. If she reaches out first to you, this may be revealing her outgoing nature as well as suggesting that she knows what she wants. If she places her hand on the bottom of yours during the handshake, she may want to be led.

Practice your handshakes with a friend and get your friend's reaction to your different styles. Also a gentle touch on the shoulder with a handshake may offer a feeling of, "I'm going to take care of you. You can relax. It's in my hands."

Warm Up Your First Appearance to Your Client's Eyes

What will your client first see when she looks at you? The most important sign of your warmth is a friendly smile. Even when you are just walking through the reception area be well aware that first impressions are taking place. Of course, it goes without saying that you are a model of your salon's work, and a neat look coupled with a warm, welcoming smile in addition to your caring handshake are guaranteed winners. Well-ironed clothes reveal your attention to detail, which reassures your client that you will pay attention to every detail of the style you give her. A salon uniform connotes professionalism, while a well-coordinated outfit suggests an eye on fashion and attention to detail.

Warm Up Your First Words to Your Client's Ears

"Hello, Mrs. Williams, Welcome to Stage Right. I'm Melissa."

Couple this greeting with the perfect handshake and a warm, cheery smile and you are making first impressions on the client's ears, eyes and touch. Research indicates that when we use a client's name we have their full attention for a full 5 to 7 seconds. Whenever making an important point always use your client's name immediately before making your point. The more difficult the person's name is, the more opportunity you have to show her that you care and you are attuned to details. Ask her to pronounce it, in some cases to spell it, and repeat it until she smiles. It is likely rare for her to receive this kind of attention. Anyone with a difficult name doesn't hear her name as often since others are afraid of getting it wrong, so they avoid saying it. You are different. You are a Psy-Cosmetologist!

Once again, you are encouraged to practice your First Impression Skills with your friends and you will experience yourself growing more confident and more successful.

Who do you know who gives a great first impression upon meeting them? What do they do that you can use?

_____

_____

Warm Up Your Non-Verbal Communication with Your Client

We communicate through our words and through our body language. In fact, it has been demonstrated by the non-verbal communication expert Albert Mehrabian that we are perceived in three ways:

• 55 percent visually, or our body language

• 38 percent vocally, or our tone of voice

• 7 percent verbally, or our spoken words

This is known as the 7/38/55 rule.

Imagine, only 7 percent of our message is received through our actual words, and 93% is received through our body language and tone of voice!

Non-verbal communication is how people communicate, intentionally and unintentionally, without words.

Non-verbal communication is how people communicate, intentionally and unintentionally, without words. This may include our facial expressions, body positions and movement, tone of voice, gestures and gaze.

Consider how some emotions are revealed without saying a word. The challenge is that often we are giving off a negative impression without knowing it. Here are a few turn-offs.

1. Hands on hips when speaking or listening is a confrontational stance. We are making ourselves wider or bigger, communicating, "Bring it on. I'm ready for you!"

2. Raised eyebrows indicate a person is in a judgmental mood.

3. Anger is expressed by a narrowing of our eyes, lowering our eyebrows and putting our mouths in a straight thin line.

4. Rolling our eyes clearly communicates sarcasm.

In his brilliant book, *Maximum Influence*, Kurt W. Mortensen describes the power of our hands in communication. He concludes:

"The way we use our hands tells others a lot about what we are thinking and feeling. For example, if your hands are tucked away in your pocket or behind your back, you may be perceived as holding something back. Clenched fists may portray anger or tension. Holding your hands around your face - over your mouth, by your ear, etc. - may portray dishonesty. Stroking your chin shows you are thinking about what has been said. If you place your hands flat on the table in front of you, you may be sending a signal that you agree. On the other hand, placing your hands on your hips may express defiance or dominance. "

Mortensen offers some thoughts about how a person's head may indicate what the person is thinking about the message of another.

- If we tilt our head towards another it sends a message we are interested in their message.
- Tilting our head away, or looking around the room, reveals our lack of interest.
- Resting our hand on our head indicates boredom.
- Nodding the head suggests that you are interested in what they are saying.
- Pointing our feet in the direction of the other, we are indicating our interest.
- Pointing our feet "away" sends a message of disagreement.
- Foot tapping reveals boredom.
- When a person leans towards another, she is feeling closer.
- A relaxed posture is telling the world we are open.
- Hands in back of our head shouts that we are either arrogant or defiant.
- Fidgeting demonstrates that we are nervous or tense.

Low First Impression Skills	Medium First Impression Skills	High First Impression Skills
Gestures to client from a distance and says, "Come to the shampooing area."	Robotic self-introduction.	Gives meaningful and reassuring handshake with a smile.
Doesn't use client's name.	Uses client's name when greeting them.	Uses client's name frequently.

Tips for Improving Your First Impression Skills

1. Study your client's non-verbal communications. Remember that 93% of a message is not in the words but in the body-language and tone of voice.

2. Take every social opportunity to go out of your way introducing yourself to others making visual, auditory and tactile contact.

3. Practice communicating some of the following messages with a friend and see how accurately you can read one another's non-verbal emotions.

1) "I'm surprised"	4) "I'm disgusted"	7) "I'm shocked"
2) "I'm happy"	5) "I'm scared"	8) "I love it"
3) "I'm angry"	6) "I'm judging you"	9) "I'm thinking"

If you've found these ideas meaningful, consider reading the book *Maximum Influence* by Kurt W. Mortensen.

For any questions, further dialogue, or challenges with material in this chapter, please email us at howardh@peoplemediainc.com.

Chapter 13
Bonding Skills: Connect with People

When we find we have things in common with other people, it brings us closer to them. Each connection reveals that we are similar in some and perhaps even many ways. This gives us things to talk about that we both are interested in. In those moments of making similarity connections, we are using our "Bonding Skills." Bonding Skills involve connecting with your client through areas of agreement and common links. Bonding Skills have the ability to make connections with people by finding similarities and staying in the agreement mode.

> *Bonding Skills involve connecting with your client through areas of agreement and common links.*

The similarity-attraction effect reveals that the more we think someone is similar to us, the more we tend to like her. It makes sense. If you and I meet in Australia and find that we are both from the United States, then Pennsylvania, we have an immediate connection. We will also start to subconsciously conclude a whole host of things about each other.

Joy, a Baltimore stylist, immediately bonds with everyone she meets. In a short period of time, you feel like you have known her for years. Joy quickly zeroes in on things she has in common with people and can even turn areas of disagreement into agreements. When you are throwing a party, you want to make sure Joy is there, because with her the party will be a success. She has a natural sense of finding similarities between herself and others. Joy is most certainly a Psy-Cosmetologist.

Who do you know who has Bonding Skills like Joy?

_____

_____

Positive people have the skills to connect instantly with others in a way that subtly communicates, "We are alike." By the end of a party, the positive person has circulated throughout the room and has everyone feeling that they have known her for years. These skills of connection with others are Bonding Skills.

Bonding Skills can be demonstrated in a variety of ways. In this chapter, we will discuss some types of Bonding Skills: (1) listening for similarities between yourself and the other person, (2) finding areas of agreement, even in disagreements, (3) getting people into a "yes" mood, (4) making "we" references, (5) starting with "and" instead of "but" when responding with a difference of opinion, (6) employing similar body language, facial gestures, and pace of speech and (7) relating to a person's unique sensory style.

1. Listening For Similarities

Immediately upon meeting someone, the positive person is scanning for ways to bond by finding similarities. Two sources of similarities include common interests and common struggles.

Common Interests

Charlie (ninth grader): "I'm really frustrated. I would like to play in the school band but my father won't let me. He thinks I should play football just because he did. Well, it's not my thing. Music is."

Tim (Psy-Cosmetologist): "You wish your father could understand what he likes isn't necessarily what you like."

Charlie: "Yeah."

Tim: "Tell me, what instrument do you play?" Charlie: "The clarinet and a little bit of saxophone."

Tim: "Wow! I never learned to play any instrument but I sure love to listen to music. Could you bring your clarinet into the salon one day and play something for me?"

Charlie: "Sure."

Tim: "What is your favorite song to play?" Charlie: "I have lots of favorites. What's yours?"

Tim's interest in music helped Charlie to re-energize his interest. Charlie thinks that maybe his liking of music is okay. After all, if Tim, who as a Psy-Cosmetologist always knows what to say, has a similar interest, he himself can't be that strange. Whether or not his father allows Charlie to pursue his love of music, Charlie knows that he can drop his mask in front of at least one adult.

Common Struggles

Al (high school student): "I applied to six colleges that I really wanted to get into and was turned down by each."

Stacy (Psy-Cosmetologist): "That's really frustrating for you, huh!" (empathy) Al: "Sure is. I don't know what I'm going to do with myself."

Stacy: "You know, Al, I really wanted to be an artist at one time but I lived too far from any big cities to make any contacts. I dreamt, slept, and constantly thought about it, but I didn't want to move away from my family and it seemed impossible."

Al: "What did you do?"

Stacy: "I considered other jobs that would allow me to be creative and applied to beauty school. This career is fulfilling for me in the same way being an artist would be, and I can continue to live close to my family."

Al: "Well, maybe I can apply to a few other colleges and if I still don't succeed, find out what else I can do."

Al found out that Stacy was just like him in a way. She, too, experienced disappointment in her lifetime and wasn't devastated by it. She demonstrated to Al that there was still hope and many alternatives. She didn't tell Al what to do, but through her own experiences she helped Al see that he doesn't have to be perfect to be accepted. Perhaps Al previously didn't want to let his uncle down by admitting the rejections. Now he was free of that burden.

2. Finding Areas Of Agreement, Even In Disagreement

Besides listening for commonalities between yourself and others, another bonding skill is to find areas of agreement, even when disagreeing about an issue. The idea that opposites attract, while true in the physical sciences, is quite false in the science of human relations. While long-lasting relationships have some differences on the surface ("She's outgoing, I'm quiet"), at a deeper level they are quite similar ("We both believe trust is important in a relationship").

> *Agreement skills involve getting people into an agreement mode.*

Agreement skills involve getting people into an agreement mode. The Psy-Cosmetologist is constantly listening with an ear toward finding areas in which all sides agree. This is especially useful during strong disagreements.

Notice how Betty focuses on an area where she agrees with her client Joan:
Joan: "You think the government isn't doing enough to help the needy, and I think that creates a dependency on the government."

Betty: "Then we both agree that things as they are aren't working, don't we?"
Joan: "Absolutely."

Agreement skills can also be used in a rather curious and creative way when dealing with a hostile person's direct attack. Take some time to sense Bill's use of agreement skills with Ed:

Ed: "I think you are a real phony." Bill: "I agree."

Ed: "I agree that you think I'm a phony. We are in agreement. We both agree that you think I'm a phony. And I think it is only fair that if I agree that you think I'm a phony, then you will agree that I don't think I'm a phony!"

A Psy-Cosmetologist can comfortably agree with a person who disagrees with him or her. In other words, when in a disagreement with someone, practice reflecting what the other person is saying and adding that you agree that is the way the other person feels. After all, aren't they the top expert on how they feel? Asking for advice on how you can improve also disarms any person just simply trying to bring you down.

3. Getting People Into a "Yes" Mood

The positive person orchestrates an upbeat rhythm in all relationships, skillfully avoiding unnecessary noise in conversations. A "yes" mood creates a tone of agreement by talking about the other person's interests and by asking questions that are likely to elicit "yes" answers.

> *A "yes" mood creates a tone of agreement by talking about the other person's interests and by asking questions that are likely to elicit "yes" answers.*

"No" is negative, isn't it? Yes, of course! Throughout our life, when we hear or see or say the word NO, we accumulate tens of thousands of negative associations. The positive person doesn't want to be linked with negative associations and carefully rephrases questions in his or her mind to bring out a "yes" response.

Stylist #1: "You don't want any products before I ring you out, do you?" Client: "Uh, no."

Stylist #2: "Did you say your name is Dina?" ("yes" question) Client: "Yes."

Stylist #2: "This conditioner is really high-quality. Does it feel soothing on your scalp?" Client: "Yes."

Stylist #2: "Would you like to take a bottle home with you today to have hair this luxurious every day?"

Client: "Yes, of course!"

Stylist #2: "Great! You will love it."

Practice phrasing questions to generate "yes" responses in others.

4. Making "We" References

To reinforce similarity and agreement, the positive person invites the other person under his or her psychological umbrella by using "we," "our," and "us" statements. "We" references communicate that you and your client feel the same way about something.

> *"We" references communicate that you and your client feel the same way about something.*

Elaine: "I hate rain!"

Rachel: "People like us prefer sunshine, don't we?" ("we" reference) Elaine: "Yes, we sure do."

5. Starting with "And" Instead of "But"

When one person makes a point and the other person responds with "but...," the first person tends to tighten, sometimes clench fists, psychologically back up, get defensive, and prepare for her own rebuttal. The person who got "butted" may not even keep listening to what the other has to say. The person with Bonding Skills knows that even when in disagreement, it is more effective to start with the word "and" instead of but. "And" keeps both parties in an agreement mood, and thus the other person will tend to listen rather than judge.

Using "and" when in disagreement takes much practice but – excuse me, I mean and – offers rich rewards. Practice by really listening to yourself say the word "but" and instead, with a big smile on your face, your head nodding in agreement, and your hands psychologically gesturing the other in, restart your response with an "and."

6. Employing Similar Body Language, Facial Gestures, and Pace of Speech

When people are in tune with each other, they will slowly gravitate to subconsciously imitate each other's mannerisms, gestures, expressions, and speech. The person with Bonding Skills does this consciously.

Remember the following ideas to slowly get in sync with others:

1. The more animated and expressive the other person is, the more animated and expressive you become.

2. The more you move your arms in a manner similar to the other person, the more the other person will feel more of a bond with you.

3. The more your facial gestures are in sync with the other person, the more the other person feels connected to you.

4. The faster or slower the other person speaks, the faster or slower you speak, and the other person will feel in rhythm with you.

Agreement Skills Make Connections and Build Bonds

Psy-Cosmetologists realize that they can have a greater impact on people when they are in agreement. Getting people into an agreement mode has the advantage of building trust and believability while communicating a sense of synchronicity. Using agreement skills also eliminates the detouring influence of disagreements between people.

7. Bonding by Relating to a Person's Sensory Representational Style

We all know that some people are right handed and some people are left handed. When bonding with people it is helpful to know that people experience their worlds differently – some are auditory, others are visual, and still others are tactile or kinesthetic. These are there sensory representational styles. Our sensory representational style is the way we represent our world to ourselves. There are three most frequent ways of connecting our message with another – we can get the visual to **see** our point of view, or get the auditory to **hear** us, or we could get in **touch** with the tactile person.

> *Our sensory representational style is the way we represent our world to ourselves.*

When we take a moment to sense a person's representation style, we can connect with her in her primary way of experiencing life. Our sensory representational style is the primary sense we most frequently use to represent the world to ourselves. For example, a visual person primarily represents the world to himself in pictures and images [visual bias], while an auditory person represents the world to himself through words and sounds [auditory bias]. How do you recognize a person with an auditory bias?

Serving Clients with an Auditory Bias

> *A client with an auditory bias has a tendency to experience the world through spoken words and sounds.*

A client with an auditory bias has a tendency to experience the world through spoken words and sounds. Words and sounds stimulate auditory sensations in the person's mind. The auditory person's highs and lows are related to sounds. The auditory person has a stronger reaction to loud sounds or disharmonious words and auditory distractions than others. Auditories are the first ones to capture a sound in the background and ask, "Did you hear that?" They also love the words and melody of the music in the background and are moved by romantic words in a song or a lover's soft voice.

Select your words wisely when talking to an auditory person. For example, words and phrases like "listen," "hear," "harmonize," "tune in," "clear as a bell," and "loud and clear" appeal to a person with an auditory bias. And when someone tells you that your idea "sounds good," or says, "I hear you," you know that you are with an auditory person.

Prepare your presentation in a way that appeals to a person with an auditory bias. For example, it wouldn't be as effective presenting a product with the words, "**See** what I mean," as it would be to ask, "Does that **sound** good?"

• Practice listening for clients who have an auditory bias. They love words, sounds, music, and would rather listen to a tape than read a book.

• An auditory person's speech is slow, organized, clear and articulate.

• During your presentation, ask, "Do you hear what I'm saying?" or "Does that sound about right?"

• Speak with rhythm, because a monotone voice turns an auditory off.

• Use alliteration whenever possible. Alliteration creates a nice melody by offering a few words in a sentence that start with the same sounds, e.g., shiny shoes, butter biscuits, etc.

• Keep your ear to the ground and listen for clients with an auditory bias.

• Does any of this ring true to you?

• An auditory customer experiences a freezing silence in the background of a restaurant or beauty salon that isn't playing music.

• "Can't wait to hear from you!" and "Sounds good!" are typical auditory phrases. Serving Clients With a Visual Bias

> *Clients with a visual bias have a tendency to respond to words that create images, sights and pictures.*

Clients with a visual bias have a tendency to respond to words that create images, sights and pictures. Visuals use words that reveal how they represent reality to themselves. They see it. When a client listens to your presentation and responds, "I see what you mean," it is clear you are with a visual. Remember people with an auditory bias would respond, "I hear you."

Bruce was the college Romeo. He could go on and on in creating a picture in the other freshman boys' minds. One particular picture he painted I still remember. He described this girl he met from Bryn Mawr University. "Carmella has shiny coal black hair that flows down her confident shoulders. Her facial skin provides the perfect soft background for her pronounced red lips and dark mysterious eyes." That was just for starters. Bruce painted pictures and the guys in the room with a visual bias were moved.

Visual people speak faster than auditory people and consequently have a more shallow breathing pattern.

Can you picture how you would get Bruce excited about your professional offerings?

• Prepare the presentation of your product to appeal to visuals by painting pictures of your product and pictures of its benefits.

• A visual person speaks quickly (as opposed to an auditory person who speaks slowly and deliberately).

• A visual person breathes high in the chest as opposed to an auditory person who breathes from a deeper part of the chest.

• Match the breathing patterns of visuals.

• Speak faster with visual customers.

• Ask the visual questions in the way that the visual will connect with: "Is it clear to you?"
"Do you see it this way?"
"Looks good, doesn't it?"

• When leaving a visual, suggest, "I'm looking forward to seeing you again."

Serving Clients With a Tactile Bias

> *Clients with a visual bias have a tendency to approach the world through words that highlight textures and physical contact.*

Clients with a visual bias have a tendency to approach the world through words that highlight textures and physical contact. You have to get "in touch" with the tactile or the feeling person. This person's world is in slow motion because she is processing everything according to how it feels to her. The tactile person is sensitive, breathes more deeply and frequently uses many metaphors. She will talk about how things "feel," she gets a "feel" for things. And while some new ideas "look good" or "appear right" to a visual, these same ideas "sound good" to an auditory, and they "fit" or "feel right" to a tactile. Here are some common phrases you might hear from a person with a tactile bias.

"I'm grasping for something more concrete."

"I can't quite get a handle on things."

"You won't budge will you?"

And when they leave you, they leave asking you to "keep in touch."

When bonding with a tactile person, speak more slowly, match her breathing patterns and use more feeling words.

What do you think is your sensory representational style? Are you an auditory, visual, or tactile person?

_____

_____

Measuring Your Bonding Skills

Low Bonding Skills	Medium Bonding Skills	High Bonding Skills
Disagrees with the client.	Half-heartedly agrees with the client.	Constantly and creatively stays in the agreement mode.
Keeps a tone of superiority and distance.	Finds things in common with the client but still talks about differences.	Finds and focuses on all areas of similarity and agreement.

Tips for Improving Your Bonding Skills

1. Whenever meeting someone new, immediately connect with the other person by finding at least three things in common.

2. Think of someone with whom you currently disagree on an issue. Identify at least three areas in which you do agree.

3. Practice getting people into a "yes" mood by phrasing your questions in a way that people will respond with positive answers.

4. Make "we" references to the following statements;

    A. "I think that people should treat each other with respect."

    Your response: (e.g., "We..." or "People like us agree that..." or "You and I both...")

    B. "You shouldn't have to take a foreign language in school if you are never going to use it."

    Your response:

C. "I love the Dallas Cowboys!"

Your response:

5. Resist responding to someone you disagree with by starting with the word "but." Instead, start with the word "and" to stay in the agreement mode.

6. Take every social interaction as an opportunity to practice mirroring a person's body language, facial gestures, and pace of speech.

7. With which style would each of the following statements be most effective?
A. Auditory
B. Visual
C. Tactile

1.____ "This professional product will feel great on your hair."

2.____ "You'll look great with this style."

3.____ "Do you have a feel for this?"

4.____ "You'll hear a lot of compliments with this color."

5.____ "Does that ring a bell?"

6.____ "Do you see what I mean about how to give your hair more shine?"

7.____ "How about a new look?"

8.____ "Does that sound good?"

9.____ "This new look will fit nicely into your plans for the wedding."

10.____ "You'll see a change in your hair immediately."

Answers. 1 C, 2 B, 3C 4A, 5A, 6B, 7B, 8A, 9B,10B

If you've found these ideas meaningful, consider reading the book *Instant Rapport* by Michael Brooks.

For any questions, further dialogue, or challenges with material in this chapter, please email us at howardh@peoplemediainc.com.

Chapter 14
Empathizing Skills: Sense Feelings

It is so rewarding when we are with someone who understands how we are feeling, isn't it? When we are with them, we feel safe to open up and share our experiences with them. In these special moments, we are with a person who has "Empathizing Skills." Empathizing Skills involve listening for the feelings underneath your client's words.

> *Empathizing Skills involve listening for the feelings underneath your client's words.*

Real contact with another person is perhaps one of the most exciting things we can experience in life. That contact is real communication. Communication is the most vital component in the stylist-client relationship. A stylist **cannot not communicate** with her client. Silence communicates as strongly as continuous talk. The way the stylist touches, moves, and responds communicates a message. Clients often choose their stylists based on their communication skills.

This chapter is designed to help you communicate more empathetically to turn your clients ON. By using Empathizing Skills, you will be a person whom clients want to be with all the time. Through learning Empathizing Skills, you can learn to feel comfortable with almost any person at any time and can know how to listen and really understand them. Empathy skills can also help you avoid the trap of feeling you have to solve people's problems.

Compare these different stylist's responses to a client's statement:

Client: Guess what, I became a grandmother last week!

Stylist #1: Oh, that's nothing – *I* have been a grandmother ten times already. Let *me* tell you about *my* grandchildren.

Stylist #2: A grandmother for the first time! How exciting that must be for *you*. Can *you* bring in a picture of *your* grandchild next time?

Which stylist has better Empathizing Skills? If both of these example stylists have equal cutting abilities, which one do you think will have a bigger following? The answer, obviously, is the second stylist. The second stylist has Empathizing

Skills, the single most person-centered skill for success. Just count the number of I's and MEs in the first example and the number of YOUs and YOURs in the second!

In this chapter on Empathizing Skills you will find yourself developing your skills in listening and responding.

With empathy, you will not only be more effective and popular with clients, but also with your coworkers, family, and friends.

What is Empathy?

Empathy is the generous and rare gift of seeing the world through the eyes of another, hearing the world through the ears of another, and feeling the world through the heart of another. You could say that empathy is walking a mile in another person's shoes. Empathy is the skill of really listening to understand another's feelings. Empathetic communication is the skill of responding in a way that communicates that you understand those feelings.

Another way to perceive this important skill of empathy is to contrast what empathy is with what empathy isn't.

What Empathy Is	What Empathy Is Not
1) Empathy is trying to understand someone's feelings.	1) Empathy is not trying to outdo someone by playing "Can you top this?" with them.
2) Empathy is understanding the perspective of another person.	2) Empathy is not judging people.
For example:	For example:
Client: My husband is a Republican	Client: My husband is a Republican

What Empathy Is	What Empathy Is Not
and I am a Democrat.	and I am a Democrat.
Stylist: Sounds like things get kind of prickly around election time!	Stylist: I agree with your husband.
3) Empathy is communicating your another person's problems.	3) Empathy is not trying to solve client's feelings back to them.

Add some of your own ideas about what empathy is and is not. Consider things like how you can tell when people are in tune with you, and how you can tell when they aren't. Include factors like the way they look, their body language, mannerisms, and what they say.

Measuring a Stylist's Levels of Empathy

There are good cuts and bad cuts. There are both good and bad ways to communicate. The great news is that we are also able to measure good Empathizing Skills.

To measure Empathizing Skills, take a look at the Stylist Empathy Rating Scale. Evaluate the responses that follow from a low-level response (poor communication) to an ultimate high level of empathetic communication.

In the next few minutes, you will understand exactly what it is that effective communicators know and do.

Stylist Empathy Rating Scale

Low Empathy Skills	High Empathy Skills
No stylist-client interaction except "How do you want your hair cut?"	Stylist listens for the client's feelings and shares them. By being understood at a feeling level, client feels comfortable, safe, and trusting. The stylist now learns more about the client's lifestyle and can make better recommendations. Stylist earns the right to be a consultant to the client's cosmetology needs.
Stylist talks about externals – soaps, weather, etc.	
Fringe contact with client.	
Stylist talks about self – "What you said reminds me...	
Stylist talks more than 80% of the time.	
Stylist judges – "You're right" or "You're wrong."	

Study the scale until you are ready to rate some typical stylist responses to client statements. Notice that high responses – the best – include identifying the feelings behind the client's words and sharing them.

Imagine a person saying the same thing to two different stylists and receiving two different answers. Go back to your rating scale and give each stylist response an empathetic communications rating.

Client: I'm afraid of having my hair colored. I don't know how my husband will take to it. Stylist #1: Oh, that reminds me of the time that my husband told me what to do and I told him where to go.

Your rating (LOW or HIGH Empathy?)_____

Stylist #2: Like all good, new experiences, the first time somebody gets color, it's a bit scary. You're feeling a little anxious about how your husband will respond. But underneath, you sound as if you could get excited about a new look. Perhaps your husband will sense your excitement.

Your rating (LOW or HIGH Empathy?)_____

Just as you learn to master texturing or coloring, you can master empathy. It may be a little difficult at first, but soon these skills will be an important part of your life. Let's look at your ratings.

Notice the first stylist turned her client off by ignoring her world and immediately talking about herself. That is a low rating. Check the rating scale again to see why this response is at a low level.

The quality of the second stylist's response was rich. Notice the feeling words: "scary," "anxious," "get excited." That is a clearly empathetic response. Study these examples until you feel comfortable with the rating scale.

Listening for Feelings to Turn People On!

Obviously, by looking at the scale we can see how important it is to relate to people - not by judging, dominating, ignoring, or taking responsibility for a client's personal problems, but by tuning in to people's feelings. Most of the world does not do this, and that is why, when someone finally hears our heart, we really respond. To help you tune in to feelings, here is a list of feelings that you can use as starters:

Negative Feelings

Worried, angry, fed up, irritated, bored, confused, disappointed, worthless, disgusted, uncertain, unsure, embarrassed, humiliated, frustrated, guilty, rotten, hurt, picked on, insecure, grumpy, jealous, put down, left out, sad, unhappy, disturbed.

Positive Feelings

Respected, valued, important, appreciated, brave, confident, sure of yourself, comfortable, secure, caring, determined, encouraged, thrilled, glad, great, terrific, grateful, inspired, loved, proud, relieved, surprised, trusted.

How to Listen and Respond Empathetically

An effective way to learn to respond empathetically is to start a response off with: You feel (apply a feeling word) because (the reason).

Now here's an opportunity to develop your skill of empathy. It will be a little difficult at first, but hang in there and you will soon acquire the #1 people skill of empathy! You have studied the rating scale and have looked over a list of feeling words. Here is your chance to put to use the skill of empathetic listening and responding.

In each of the following three situations, someone says something to you. In the first case it's a client, in the second instance it is another stylist, and in the third example it is a manager.

Write what you would say back to them. Remember:

1. Look at the Empathy Rating Scale.

2. Find a feeling word from the negative or positive feelings list and select a feeling you believe the person is experiencing.

3. Keep yourself out of it. No judging.

4. Do not take responsibility to give an answer or solve someone's problem. Simply share a feeling that you think they may be experiencing.

Client says to you: It was our fifth wedding anniversary yesterday and my husband didn't even remember.

Respond: (Check rating scale; find a feeling from the negative or positive list of feelings.)

You feel _____

... because _____

Another stylist says to you: I used to feel important around here until this new stylist came. Now the manager spends so much time with her.

Respond:

You feel _____

... because _____

Manager says to you: I'm really in the middle. The owner puts pressure on me, and you guys seem to be ganging up on me. I don't know what to do – it's not like before when I was styling. Since I got the promotion, I've lost all my friends here.

Respond:

You feel _____

... because _____

Do all of your answers include feeling words? Did you stay on the topic? Did you keep yourself out? Did you avoid giving advice or judging? If so, great job!

If not, take a few seconds and write a different response. You can do it!

Congratulations! You have just learned the most important skill that people who work with people need – empathy. Empathy Vs. Apathy and Sympathy

Don't make your livelihood more demanding than it is. Avoid burnout by communicating with Empathizing Skills, and avoid both the apathy and sympathy traps.

Clients, like stylists, have families, friends, joys, and problems. In a world that frequently doesn't seem to care, almost anyone who finds even a slightly open door to bring his or her problems through will do so.

Sometimes without even knowing it, people burden others. This is especially true of some salon clients who feel close to their stylists in that special ongoing relationship. The close contact between stylist and client involves human touch and even "washing the mask away." The salon provides an atmosphere that sends out a natural invitation for a person to unload. A client can get her hair done by a caring individual who also takes the time to understand her feelings.

In this chapter on listening and responding, it becomes vital to understand what effective, empathetic listening is, as well as what it is not. The right kind of listening – empathetic listening – builds a relationship between client and stylist and is a very important human-relations skill. But the wrong kind of listening – apathetic or sympathetic – either destroys relationships or puts the stylist in a role he or she isn't prepared for. Before we discuss effective listening, let's examine the two ineffective listening and responding styles.

Apathetic-Responding Stylist

Client: I know I don't have an appointment and you're booked solid, but I'd like to get highlights because I'm going to see my son tomorrow. He's coming home from the service, and I haven't seen him in almost two years.

Stylist (Apathetic response): I don't have any time.

The stylist totally ignores the client's personal concerns and feelings. There are obviously some real emotions that this woman is experiencing, and the stylist sweeps them under the rug. It certainly wouldn't be hard for an empathetic stylist to win this client over, would it? Why? The stylist missed her feelings, the point of Psy-Cosmetology.

Sympathetic over-involvement, the next type of response, is the opposite of apathetic non-caring.

Sympathetic-Responding Stylist

Client: I know I don't have an appointment and you are booked solid, but I'd like to get highlights because I'm going to see my son tomorrow. He's coming home from the service, and I haven't seen him for almost two years.

Stylist (Sympathetic response): I had a class I was going to tonight, but I'll cancel and do your hair. I'll even bake you a cake for him tomorrow. The highlights are on me.

The main reason stylists burn out on the job, go home, shut off their cell phone, and close themselves off from the outside world is that they over-invest themselves with by listening and responding sympathetically to people.

The cosmetologist takes a huge burden off her own shoulders the minute she clearly faces this fact: "While I solve hair problems, I do not have to solve my client's personal problems; it is not my responsibility."

But then, what do you do when people bring their problems to you? There is a perfect answer: Empathizing Skills.

Empathetic-Responding Stylist

Client: I know I don't have an appointment and you are booked solid, but I'd like to get highlights because I'm going to see my son tomorrow. He's coming home from the service, and I haven't seen him for almost two years.

Stylist (Empathetic response): You must feel really **excited** (a feeling word) about seeing your son after almost two years. I'll bet you can't wait. Let me check my book to see if there is any possible way I can give you highlights. . . I'm sorry, Mrs. Smith, I can't. I know that must be really *disappointing* (another feeling word) to you. Maybe April or Darren can fit a highlighting in tomorrow.

Empathetic responding involves tuning in to a person's feelings. The reasons a stylist uses empathetic responding are:

1. It builds rapport
2. When a client feels a good, safe relationship, she shares more about herself, which aids in understanding her lifestyle, thus enabling the stylist to better understand the client's cosmetic needs.

Two Stylist-Client Dialogues Comparing Sympathetic Vs. Empathetic Listening and Responding

Sympathetic-Responding Stylist

Client: My husband is in danger of losing his job.

Sympathetic stylist: Well, let me see if I know anyone who is hiring. Client: And my teenager is having a problem at school.

Sympathetic stylist: Did you talk to the principal? Client: No.

Sympathetic stylist: What about his teacher? Client: No.

Sympathetic stylist: Well, I know the school counselor. Let me talk to her.

Client: My in-laws are coming for dinner Sunday, and I just feel so inferior about my cooking. Sympathetic stylist: I'm baking lasagna Saturday. Let me bring you some.

Empathetic-Responding Stylist

A person with high Empathizing Skills understands and shares back the feelings of another person – but stops there.

Observe how an empathetic stylist would listen to the same client.

Client: My husband is in danger of losing his job.

Empathetic stylist: You feel **a little uneasy** now, I guess, because of your husband's uncertain future at work.

Client: And my teenager is having a problem at school.

Empathetic stylist: You're **worried** about Jimmy.

Client: I've been so depressed lately.

Empathetic stylist: Sounds like you are going through **a little bit of a slump**. I'll bet you're waiting for things to turn around.

Client: Yeah.

Empathetic stylist: Maybe we can start here, with a new style. That will give you a lift!

Notice that the stylist did not get caught in the "solve my problem" trap but just **listened for feelings** – even more effective, without the emotional drain.

The three listening styles are contrasted below:

Apathetic Listening: Communicating that I am not interested in your feelings or your life. I'm just here to cut your hair.

Empathetic Listening: Communicating (without saying it, of course) that I am interested in understanding your feelings and sharing them with you. Yet I am fully aware that they are not my feelings and your world is not my world. We are two different people, and I can't possibly solve ten people's personal problems each day.

Sympathetic Listening: Communicating that not only am I interested in understanding your feelings and your world, but I'm going to solve your problems, and if I don't, I'll feel guilty.

Deeper Empathy

Along with emphatically sensing the feelings of another person by observing her words and body language, sometimes we can sense a deeper empathic state. This deeper empathic state involves sensing what the person isn't saying.

Deeper empathy is best revealed by the words of a poem I read years ago. I could not identify the author, but the words open our eyes to a person who is sometimes a challenge.

Please Hear What I Am Not Saying

Don't be fooled by me

Don't be fooled by the face I wear.

For I wear a mask. I wear a thousand masks. Masks that I'm afraid to take off.

And none of them are me.

Pretending is an art that's second nature with me, But don't be fooled,

For god's sake don't be fooled.

I give you the impression that I'm secure.

That all is sunny and unruffled with me, Within as well as without.

That confidence is my name and coolness my game, That water's calm and I'm in command,

And that I need no one. But don't believe me,

Please,

My surface may seem smooth, but my surface is my mask, My ever-varying and ever-concealing mask. Beneath lies no smugness, no complacence. Beneath dwells the real me in confusion, in fear,

In aloneness. But I hide this.

I don't want anybody to know it.

I panic at the thought of my weakness and fear being exposed. That's why I frantically create a mask to hide behind.

A nonchalant, sophisticated facade, to help me pretend

To shield me from the glance that knows. But such a glance is precisely my salvation,

My salvation, and I know it.

That is, if it's followed by acceptance. If it's followed by love.

It's the only thing that can liberate me from myself,

From my own self-built prison walls,

From the barriers that I so painstakingly erect.

It's the only thing that will assure me of what I cannot assure myself, That I am really worth something.

But I don't tell you this, I don't dare. I'm afraid to.

I'm afraid your glance will not be followed by acceptance and love. I'm afraid that deep down I'm nothing.

That I'm no good,

And that you will see this and reject me. So I play my game,

My desperate pretending game, With a facade of masks,

That glittering but empty parade of masks. And my life becomes a front.

I idly chatter to you in the suave tones of surface talk. I tell you everything that's really nothing,

And nothing of what's everything, Of what's crying within me.

So when I'm through my routine –

Don't be fooled by what I'm saying.

Please listen carefully, and hear what I'm Not saying.

What I'd like to be able to say, What for survival I need to say, But what I can't say.

I dislike hiding. Honestly.

I dislike the superficial game I'm playing.

The superficial, phony game.

I really like to be genuine and spontaneous, And me, but you've got to help me.

You've got to hold out your hand,

Even when that's the last thing I seem to want, or need.

Only you can wipe away from my eyes the blank stare of the breathing dead.

Only you can call me into aliveness.

Each time you're kind, and gentle, and encouraging,

Each time you try to understand because you really care, My heart begins to grow wings, very small wings,

Very feeble wings. But wings.

With your sensitivity and sympathy

And your power of understanding, You can breathe life into me.

I want you to know that.

I want you to know how important you are to me.

How you can be a creator of the person that is me, If you choose to,

Please choose to.

You alone can break down the wall behind which I tremble, You alone can remove my mask,

You alone can release me from my shadow-world of panic and uncertainty, From my lonely prison.

So do not pass me by. Please do not pass me by. It will not be easy for you,

A long conviction of worthlessness builds strong walls.

The nearer you approach to me, the blinder I may strike back.

It's irrational, but despite what the books may say about man, I am irrational. I fight against the very thing I cry out for.

But I am told that love is stronger than strong walls, And in this lies my hope.

My only hope.

Please try to beat down those walls with firm hands.

But with gentle hands. Who am I, you may wonder?

I am someone you know very well.

For I am every man and woman you meet.

– Anonymous

When a Psy-Cosmetologist is aware of the deeper feelings under a person's behavior, he or she can respond to these deeper feelings. For example, underneath anger is always the feeling of hurt or fear. The stylist, then, can deal with the hurt or fear, instead of getting angry themselves at their angry client.

Tips for Improving Your Empathizing Skills

1. The next time you are in a situation where you feel insecure about not having an answer to someone's problem, feel secure that it's not your responsibility. Simply share with her the feelings behind her words. Feel good!

2. The next time you are in a situation with a client where you feel apathetic, simply listen for feelings and share them back. You'll see how simple it is. Feel good!

3. Since clients choose their stylists based upon empathy as well as technical skill, the skill of responding to feelings is the key to turning people on. Feel good!

Now, let's see how you can take your turned-on clients to new levels with your Specializing Skills!

For any questions, further dialogue, or challenges with material in this chapter, please email us at howardh@peoplemediainc.com.

"Specializing Skills involve communicating, 'You are special,
have so much going for you, and I enjoy being with you,' to your client
through your words and actions."

Chapter 15
Specializing Skills: Experience Everyone As Important

Specializing Skills involve communicating, "You are special,
have so much going for you, and I enjoy being with you," to
your client through your words and actions.

In what relationships do you feel respected and important? In these
relationships - you are experiencing people who have "Specializing Skills."
Specializing Skills involve communicating, "You are special, have so much going
for you, and I enjoy being with you," to your client through your words and
actions.

The new economy is reflected in the fact that we consumers are more conscious than ever of where we will spend our hard earned money. We have many choices and can leave one professional or business and find another one. It wasn't too long ago that my parents would have never, ever left their church. Today it is common to change churches because of the new minister, or priest. Patients, depending on the limitations of their medical plan, will change doctors and even search out different hospitals. Do you see the billboards advertising to "get your surgery with us, because we care?" My own profession of psychotherapy is scrutinized by patients on the Internet for how much care they are shown during their sessions. Have you noticed the rapid proliferation of charter schools because some public schools have lost touch with today's assertive public? Your field of cosmetology is especially being impacted by the new economy as well. We can look at this new discerning client as either a problem or an opportunity, based upon whether we prepare for them or go about business the same way as a decade ago. The fact that 96% of dissatisfied customers to any business do not tell the business and instead just leave tells us that for every client who complains, there are 25 others who never said a word (except on-line)!

A Special Way of Dealing with Today's Demanding Clients

So how do we prepare for this new assertive client, patient or customer? Let's look around and notice something positive going on in all professions. This difference that makes the difference is a positive, special approach to people. In medicine the positive-focusing fruits are appearing on the trees of the profession. Holistic medicine is calling for "personal responsibility for one's medical self." Doctors are talking about the curative powers of the human body, coupled with the human mind. Did you know that there is a positive cholesterol, one that is good for you? In addition to sickness clinics, wellness clinics have been emerging throughout the more advanced nations. The scales of medicine are making dramatic shifts, influenced by the new economy. To whom would you rather go: a doctor who tells you how sick you look, focuses on all the things that are wrong with you, or a doctor who sees all the assets in your body, the strengths you have to cope with disease, and helps you develop a positive wellness-keeping plan?

Serving today's demanding and aware clients is an idea whose time has come to psychology as well. As we mentioned before, Positive Psychology is rapidly replacing the sickness and disease model of the past. Therapy visits have much more of a focus on finding the patient's strengths rather than their deficiencies. Counseling sessions do not dwell on the unchangeable past but on helping the patient mobilize her strengths to create a better future for herself.

When I work with schools, teachers are craving a more positive way of motivating their students, encouraging them to realize what's right, not what's wrong with them.

And have you noticed churches slowly changing emphasizing good news, rather than motivating people with the fear of hell?

And have you observed how nice and sensitive librarians are today? Quite a change from the past, when the librarian would stare at you disapprovingly over her glasses when your book was returned a day late?

Even the Department of Motor Vehicles is becoming a less painful place to wait in line.

Can you think of any businesses that didn't make it because of poor service? Name a place that you feel has very good service. What do you like about it?

My Dentist Got It!

I had a few interesting experiences with dentists in my early years. Although it is assumed that a dentist's responsibility is to find dental problems, the manner in which the dentist relays that message to the client is crucial. Dentists would dwell on my cavity, my tooth problems, and concentrate only on what was wrong, not what was right. As a teen, I cringed when dentists would give me sermons about my cavity, or ask me such embarrassing questions as, "Don't you brush or floss?" in front of the dental assistants.

A few years later, after having "given up" on dentists, I was talking to a gentleman I had just met at a cocktail party, and he said, "You have great teeth." I said, "What?!" He said, "You have fine looking teeth." I was totally taken back by that. Later in our conversation, I asked him what he did for a living. He said, "I'm a dentist." I immediately asked him for his business card and made an appointment for the following week. In only four visits, all of my problems were treated, and every six months I return to this positive, asset-focusing dentist. Because of his positive approach, I looked forward to seeing him. The good doctor's positive approach to patients is attracting the assertive consumer of today.

Now to the real point of this chapter on the importance of Specializing Skills in the salon. If increasingly we find physicians looking for people's physical wellness, educators tuning in to students' positive learning potentials, and dentists emphasizing patients' healthy teeth and focusing on preventative dentistry, how do the hundreds of thousands of people in the beauty profession need to shift their thinking?

Reaching for the Assets in the Client's Hair, Skin, and Nails

I am fascinated with how much of a stylist's time is spent talking about problems in the client's hair. In fact, it is common to hear, "You have a problem with dandruff," or "Your hair is unusually oily," or "Your split ends are quite noticeable." It is so second nature that many stylists think nothing of it. However, when we asked hairstylists how these same sentences felt when they listened to them empathetically from the client's point of view, and experienced them sometimes within ear's range of other patrons a little uneasy.

I am not addressing this touchy issue to put anyone down; that approach is never helpful. And neither could I say that it is wrong for anyone to focus on the problems, because I was more guilty than anyone spending eight hours a day in my past practice talking about problems. This was the way my profession, the medical profession, the teaching profession was trained.

Cosmetology school textbooks appropriately have one or more chapters on "diseased hair" in its various forms, but no chapters on assets in hair. So, just as the old-time psychiatrist looked for disease or "What's wrong here?," hairstylists stroked through a client's hair with antennae extended to spot the problems. And, unfortunately, like the old-time psychiatrist's limited goal of helping the person progress from a diseased to a "normal" state, the stylist's highest goal was to make the hair normal. But, normal is not a very exciting description for a person's hair in the beauty industry, is it?

Kathy Develops Salon Phobia

The effects of these "evil eyes" in all professions, especially the cosmetology profession, was dramatically driven home to me one autumn Saturday afternoon as I listened to one salon client, Kathy S., tell us of her past salon experiences. The 31-year-old blonde sales manager told us about how she had been totally turned of by the inhumane, negative treatment she received in most of her salon experiences as a child and a teenager.

Kathy explained, "Ever since I was a young child, I would go to the salon and get abused verbally by the hairdressers. I would be told repeatedly that I have 'baby fine, limp hair' that could never be permed, and never be allowed to grow long. One guy told me that my hair looked like h---! It happened over and over again. How do you think it made me feel? I mean, that stuff they're talking about is growing out of my head!

"Whenever I would go anywhere, I would feel so self-conscious about my baby hair. I felt so inferior to everyone else. And strangely, my hair inferiority came from the place you'd least expect – from my hairdresser. My mother would actually have to reassure me after I got out of the salon that it wasn't as bad as they told me. So, I'd change salons and hear from someone else, "There's not much we can do with hair like yours. But, we'll do the best we can." After years of hearing what's wrong with my hair, I decided to cut my own hair. So I saved myself hundreds and hundreds of dollars, and I didn't have to be reminded about my baby hair."

Meeting Tommy, the Psy-Cosmetologist

Then a smile broke out on her beautiful face as she went on – "When I was twenty- seven, I decided to give the salon one more try when I heard about this positive and sensitive man named Tommy, a stylist in northern New Jersey. After arriving at the salon, I was escorted to his chair and my tension was already building. As he came over to me with a big smile on his face, I spoke first and apologetically wished him good luck with this mess on my head. He stopped me in the middle of the apology and said, 'Kathy, you have such a gorgeous face and beautiful cheekbones.' While running his fingers through my hair he added, 'Your hair is like silk. Cutting it will be a breeze.' He discussed all of my special features that even I was unaware of. He helped me realize all of my hair's potential.

"A few appointments later, Tommy even encouraged me to let him highlight my hair. He showed me how to take care of my hair, to respect it, to be proud of it. Not only did he change my hair, he changed my perspective. I totally trusted him. I felt like a winner in his presence because I knew that he liked and respected my hair, and me. I would not have had the guts to apply for this sales manager's job without having found Tommy. And, interestingly, my job promotion located me in Wilmington, Delaware. But every five weeks I travel four hours to see Tommy."

Doesn't what Kathy, the salon client, said make sense? Are we not more attracted to people who respect us and see what is right with us? In the Human Revolution, in any profession, the successful experts will be those who are not only experts in their technical areas, but also experts in understanding people. And the first principle in understanding people is knowing that people favor the positives about themselves over the negatives. Don't you?

The REACH Concept (Relating by Emphasizing the Assets in Your Client's Hair)

Kathy is not alone. After several dozen interviews with salon clients, I found negative focusing to be a common experience in the discussions stylists had with their clients. As a result, I began addressing a dramatic shift in the way cosmetologists relate with their clientele. In an address delivered in Des Moines, Iowa, I suggested –

"I would like to discuss a concept barely addressed before. It appears that the cosmetology profession is sitting on the welcome mat of a brand new future in terms of the way professional relate to their clients. The old style of relating to the disease and deficiencies of the client's hair is no longer relevant in an age when we understand how people get discouraged, leave our salons, and go elsewhere. We are on the verge, I believe, of a refreshing approach to our clients, one that builds them up, builds up the assets in their hair, builds our relationship with them, and even has the subconscious effect of building our very view of ourselves.

"This new way of relating to our clients literally reaches into the assets and potential in their hair, skin, nails, physical features, and lifestyles. I would like to look at that would reach and thus call this new way of relating to clients the REACH Concept. REACH means Relating through Emphasizing the Assets in the Client's Hair first. You can REACH your clients by presenting your professional products and services in a way that benefits your clients' unique assets, strengths and potentials in his or her hair, making her feel special." At that positive moment, you are applying your Specializing Skills.

> *REACH means Relating through Emphasizing the Assets in the Client's Hair*

Think of three clients who have challenges with their hair. How could you use the REACH Concept and turn their "difficult hair" into a positive feature that you enjoy working with?

_____

_____

Specialize By Sensing Claims-to-Fames and Interests

The greatest compliment we can give to a person is by recognizing the positive uniqueness he or she has. In this world of high technology everywhere we are reduced to a number, or a service like, "Are you my 9 o'clock? Or "Are you my highlight?" In addition to helping each of your clients feel like the special person he or she is by seeing the assets and strengths in her hair, you can use your Specializing Skills to point out positive uniquenesses in their personality.

Perhaps you remember the sitcom, "Cheers," where the theme song about what attracted everyone to the bar called "Cheers."

"Making your way in the world today takes everything you got, Taking a break from all your worries, sure would help a lot. Wouldn't you like to get away sometimes you want to go

Where everybody knows your name, and there always glad you came. You want to be where you can see our troubles are all the same

You want to be where everybody knows your name."

Make it a practice to quickly find strengths, positive points, uniquenesses, dreams and client's claims-to-fames. Claims-to-fames are proud moments in peoples' lives in which they were personally proud. Many of these moments didn't matter to the rest of the world, but to the person with Specializing Skills, they take on real meaning. Find a client's claims-to-fames and you will never lose that person as a client.

Consider just a few of these subtle remarks that stands out to a Psy-Cosmetologist. Eddie, age 6: "I'm the fastest kid in first grade."

Louisa: "I'm making my special lasagna for my future in-laws." Bill: "My son Michael made the varsity football team."

Get into the other person's world using your Empathizing Skills and show your excitement by feeling what your client is feeling. Also focus on your client's interests. One practical approach some Psy-Cosmetologists use is to take a small index card, and create their

CLIENT'S INTERESTS AND CLAIMS-TO-FAME SHEET for each client. These cards include everything from knowing their sports or NASCAR heroes, to their favorite movies, books, etc. Plus this process will actually help you grow your own interests in these areas. Your excitement of being with your client will increase. And soon, imagine when your Philadelphia sports loving client comes into the salon and you greet her with, "How about those Phillies?"

Specializing Skills are the difference that makes the difference in your success with people.

Start your CLIENT'S INTERESTS AND CLAIM-TO-FAME card – think of 3 clients and write down each's interests and claims-to-fame.

Measuring Your Specializing Skills

Low Specializing Skills	Medium Specializing Skills	High Specializing Skills
Every client is treated in the same mechanized way.	Frequent or powerful clients get special treatment.	Clients see something positive and unique in every client.
No unique qualities are noticed.	. . . and all other clients blend together.	All clients feel special.

Tips for Improving Your Specializing Skills

1. Immediately spot the positive features in your client's hair, skin and nails.

2. Talk about a person's hair potential.

3. Find positive uniquenesses in your clients' personalities staying tuned to their claims-to-fames.

4. Create a small card for each client, CLIENT'S INTERESTS AND CLAIMS-TO-FAME. Simply take 5 seconds after each client noting what positive things are important in her life. Then take 5 more seconds preparing yourself to greet her the next session.

If you've found these ideas meaningful, consider reading the book *Turning People On* by Lewis Losoncy.

For any questions, further dialogue, or challenges with material in this chapter, please email us at howardh@peoplemediainc.com.

Chapter 16

Energizing Skills:
Get Excited About Your Professional Gifts

Some people have the ability to romance anything, whether it be a certain dish, a song, a car, a beauty product or a salon service. When we are excited about something we like, or have to offer our clients, we are using our "Energizing Skills." Energizing skills involve the ability to get your client excited about the new looks and benefits you and your salon have for HER.

> *Energizing skills involve the ability to get your client excited about the new looks and benefits you and your salon have for HER.*

Your client has chosen a dentist to fulfill her dental needs, and a physician to care for her medical needs. And she has chosen you to fulfill her cosmetic needs. You are the expert at fulfilling your client's cosmetic needs. Plus out of all of the salons in your area she has chosen to drive to your salon! This is a powerful statement of trust she has in you, and your salon.

You are her cosmetologist. You are not only aware of her own unique hair, skin and nail needs, but you are aware of her own unique personality through your Empathizing and Specializing Skills. You are also fully aware of all of the professional benefits, services and products that you have to offer her to fulfill her unique needs. You could say that no one is in a better position to get her excited about all the salon can offer her than you. Does that make sense? Add to that the fact that most people who are asked if they'd like to look the best they can respond with something like, "of course."

In the last chapter, we discussed how Specializing Skills are experienced when you are pointing out a client's hair, skin and nail strengths. In addition you are specializing another person when you point out positive personality characteristics, sensing her claims-to-fames and focusing on her interests. You are helping each person to experience herself as unique and special by remembering small details that you have written on your CLIENT'S INTERESTS AND CLAIMS-TO-FAME CARD.

Your Specializing Skills focus on your client's strengths. Your Energizing Skills focus on your own, and your salon's strengths, professional products and services available to benefit her. You are using your Energizing Skills when you are, first of all, getting excited about the important role you are playing in your client's beauty needs. And secondly you are developing your Energizing Skills by getting yourself and your client enthused about your professional products and services to help her look her very best. She doesn't know what you know about your salon's benefits. You do. This is your opportunity to change her life. Your enthusiasm is the most important tool for getting her excited about your salon's gifts of beauty. To understand why enthusiasm is so important let's turn to the simple idea of social comparison theory first detailed by social psychologist, Leon Festinger.

Social Comparison Theory

> *Social comparison theory is the idea that when we are in doubt about how we should feel in any situation, we look to others for the clue.*

Social comparison theory is the idea that when we are in doubt about how we should feel in any situation, we look to others for the clue. The others are usually the top experts around us in that moment.

For example the first time I flew, the flight from Philadelphia to Miami was bumpy. I didn't know whether this was unusual or not because it was my first flight. During these "bumps" I looked around the plane for the flight attendant's reactions to the roller coaster ride. She was the top expert in the area and I was in a social comparison need state. As she walked about the plane smiling, it brought a smile to my face. Her action of calmness and reassurance led to my reaction of calmness feeling reassured. She may or may not have studied social comparison theory but she certainly applied it that day to the benefits of this passenger.

There are many times we are in a state of social comparison needs watching the expert's around us. When your physician is taking your blood pressure you may be looking at her face or demeanor to get the news. If she becomes wide-eyed when she reads your pressure, it might jump even higher. If she smiles, you smile. Or how about when your specialist looks at your ex-rays or test results you wait in terror to get a glimpse of his demeanor and reaction. And whatever his reaction is, you take on that same reaction. So when people are in doubt about which emotion to experience, they look to others for the clue. You are their top expert in beauty.

Let's see how social comparison theory applies to you.

Using Your Energizing Skills to Recommend Your Professional Products and Services

Your client looks to you, as the top expert in her beauty needs, to inform her about all of the benefits your salon has to offer. Chances are she did not go to beauty school and chances are strongly that she doesn't do thirty or forty client's hair a week. And chances are that she isn't aware of all of the breakthroughs in professional beauty products and in salon services. And you probably haven't seen her at the recent hair show you went to. This is why you can give her so much more than you might realize. All she needs is your helpful beauty information coupled with your enthusiasm, or Energizing Skills for the benefits you have to offer her. Aren't you the most logical person in the world to help her look her best? How could you not be excited about that?

Applying social comparison theory to you, it appears like this. When your client is in doubt about a new product or service, she looks to you for the clue. Your words, demeanor, enthusiasm and facial reactions, like that of your doctor reading your chart, will immediately be picked up, and modeled by your client. A dull, robotic, "this product is all right, I guess," creates a dull, robotic reaction. Contrarily, a genuine testimonial like "This professional product really has great holding power that will last throughout the day," will give the clue to your client that this tube offers something she can get excited about. Isn't this exactly what the most successful salon professionals do naturally?

The psy-cosmetologist's very love of life comes through in her love of her clients, her products and services.

Developing Your Energizing Skills by Loving Your Professional Products and Services

The most effective teachers love their students, and their subject matter. The students grab hold of the teacher's enthusiasm for science or history or psychology because the teacher loves it. The best fitness teachers are enthusiastic about their classes and love offering their training programs. The most successful real-estate agents love houses and can find small, fine details to bring each home to life.

My friend Terry Tears is a Melbourne Florida carpenter. He is the best I ever met. He is an artist, a scientist and a perfectionist with wood. He not only knows wood, but he loves wood like Mother Theresa loved people. When a thrilled customer once observed, "Terry, you could have done anything you wanted to with your life," terry smiled and responded, "I know, and that's exactly what I'm doing. I love wood!" Terry loves his products and services and when he talks about what he has to offer, he is making his presentation using his Energizing Skills. And remembering social comparison theory- when people are in doubt about which emotion to experience they look to others for the clue- Terry's customers are soon loving wood too.

Practice developing your Energizing Skills about each of your professional products and services remembering that you are the expert and your client is looking to your words, facial expression and enthusiasm about each of your salon gifts. After all she doesn't know of all the ways you can help her look her best. And that's what ultimately she wants, isn't it?

What professional products and services can you get most excited about? Practice recommending these using Energizing Skills.

_____

_____

Measuring Your Energizing Skills

Low Energizing Skills	Medium Energizing Skills	High Energizing Skills
Salon has low energy.	If client is energetic, stylist will become energetic.	Stylist gets client energized about possible new looks.
Clients just want a trim.	Stylist will gladly offer new services if the client asks.	Every client is aware of all of the salon's services and products.

Tips for Improving Your Energizing Skills

1. What is your favorite professional product? Think of a client who could benefit from that product who currently isn't using it. Get your enthusiasm level up and create and practice an imaginary presentation to her, using your Energizing Skills. Remember social comparison theory and experience her smiling and getting excited about the product as well.

2. What salon service do you love offering the most? Using your Energizing Skills, build a presentation to get anybody in the whole world excited about experiencing that new style, color, highlighting, perm, manicuring, etc. Imagine even the most close-minded client in the salon opening up because of your Energizing Skills.

If you've found these ideas meaningful, consider reading the book _Passionate Salon Professionals_ by Lewis Losoncy and Joe Santy.

For any questions, further dialogue, or challenges with material in this chapter, please email us at howardh@peoplemediainc.com.

"Encouragement Skills involve the ability to help your client see her (cosmetic and life) potential and to inspire them to GO FOR IT!"

Chapter 17
Encouraging Skills: Inspire a "Go For It!" Feeling

Can you remember a time when someone had just the right words to bring out your courage to "go for it?" She made a difference, didn't she? She had "Encouragement Skills." Encouragement Skills involve the ability to help your client see her (cosmetic and life) potential and to inspire them to GO FOR IT!

Encouragement Skills involve the ability to help your client see her (cosmetic and life) potential and to inspire them to GO FOR IT!

Psychologically speaking, isn't fear one of the factors holding back your client's willingness to improve her style? Isn't the antidote to fear. . . courage? En-courage-ment is the process of bringing out your client's courage to overcome her fear of change.

Encouragement, the Ultimate Gift of the Professional Cosmetologist

In every group of people there are always a few who have a positive effect on others. You know them. They are easy to be with, are interested in others, and have a positive view of life and its possibilities. They always have their senses tuned in to find better ways. Because of their special attitudes and talents, they have the biggest impact on other people. These special people are encouragers.

Encouragement is the most effective way to bring out your clients' courage to try new looks and ideas. The average cosmetologist has studied and practiced for hundreds and hundreds of hours to refine her technical skills in cutting, coloring, and texturing. Yet very little schooling has been given to her on how to be an **encouraging hairstylist**, the key to professional – and personal – success, and, most importantly, client growth.

The Psy-Cosmetologist understands the role of client courage in her client's hairstyle change. The more one studies the importance of courage, the more one realizes that no positive change would ever be resisted if the person had courage. You could say that **encouragement is your major non-haircutting tool as a hairstylist!**

**From Discouragement to Encouragement Through You,
The Encouraging Stylist!**

The Discouraged Person...	The Encouraged Person...
1) Seeks sameness: Just a trim or "the usual."	1) Is ready for a new look!
2) Is liability-focused: "My hair is horrible."	2) Is asset-focused: "My hair has some bounce – maybe a new color would add excitement."
3) Experiences fear of change: "I don't know I'd look with a perm."	3) Is courageous: "I'll never find out what is best for me until I explore new possibilities."
4) Has low expectations and goals: "I'm happy with my hair the way it is, I guess."	4) Seeks out opportunities to exceed their own expectations: "As my stylist, what are some new ideas for my hair that you might suggest?"
5) Is closed-minded: "I've always worn my hair this way."	5) Is open-minded: "I want to look different."

The "dis-couraged" person is only one step away from looking the best she could – that one step is courage. That one step is best taken with the encouraging hairstylist!

What is Encouraging Hairstyling (EH)?

Encouraging hairstyling is a positive and easy approach to developing confident and courageous clients. The main believe behind EH is that ultimately people change their hairstyle when they themselves are motivated to change. The primary task in EH is to encourage the client's own willingness and determination to change. The raw material for EH is already there in the client in the form of her assets, resources, and potential of her hair. It is also there in her desire to look the best she possibly can. A new look encouraged by a new outlook, a rearrangement of how she views her possibilities, is what is needed. This is best achieved in the context of an encouraging relationship.

The encouraging hairstylist helps the client by first showing her what she already has going for her, then by helping her see visions and images of who she can be through your professional expertise. Finally and most important, she helps the client develop the courage to become all that she can be.

The Encouragement Hairstyling Process

Step 1: Identify Some Positive Assets, Strengths, and Resources for Potential in Your Client's Hair (Specializing). Help your client be the special person she is. An encouraging relationship is one based upon the positive. Remember, whatever you tell someone about her hair, you are telling her about herself! Always start off on a positive note, and if some negative element of the hair has to be addressed, make it a minor afterthought. Speak of it in terms of how you can improve it. Stay focused on her potential, and tie it in with her lifestyle. Keep it upbeat and positive; and show her you respect her hair, which means you respect her!

Step 2: Help People Create Visions and Images of Who He or She Can Be (Energizing). Clients are tops in your eyes! You care about her looking her best; you understand her and she trusts you. Take two sheets of paper; on one put possible styles, and on one put possible colors.

Under each, creatively list all of the service possibilities that you can give professionally to her. With her in your chair, share some new dreams, visions, and images that she can try. The more cuts and colors you show, the more panoramic the vista you open up for your client to experience. But mainly let her feel the caring behind your creative sharing. Constantly keep tying in her lifestyle. When you talk about the things you took the time to remember about her, you are giving to each of her the ultimate gift of uniqueness and to yourself the well-deserved feeling of charging her world. When you see your client's eyes flash with energy in response to a certain vision or appearance, move on to the most important step of EH.

Step 3: Help Your Client Develop the Courage to Become All That She Can Become (Encouraging). The client is special in your eyes, and you care. You have explored many new possible images with her, and she has responded to one. The only thing holding her back is. . . COURAGE. Your encouragement makes the difference. Some practical ways to encourage her include (1) helping her imagine the new look in her mind; (2) making it easy for her to see that the change is not so drastic if it really isn't; (3) helping her see how this new look is more advantageous than the current one; (4) putting the new hairstyle in the context of a new dress, a new skirt, earrings, etc.; (5) offering guarantees when relevant; (6) referring to testimonials or previous clients' experiences with this specific look; (7) discussing some significant others in her life and how they will respond positively; (8) making her enthusiastic not only with the new look but with the new "total person"; (9) helping her feel your excitement about doing the new service for her.

Feel free to add any of your own ideas on how to do Encouraging Hairstyling:

_____

_____

_____

_____

_____

Remember, To be the encouraging hairstylist, it is vital to compliment people and have the same enthusiasm after the service as you did before. If your whole salon is built on being an encouraging salon team (Part V), what an experience for a client to have – everyone supporting and encouraging the new look. And the new person!

Summary of the Encouraging Hairstylist

Courage may very well be the most important quality that a human being can have. With courage, one moves forward in life towards actualization. The encouraging hairstylist is one who sees the client in her chair, resisting becoming all that she is capable of, as simply lacking courage. The encouraging hairstylist communicates respect for her and shows caring for her as she is. The stylist helps her create visions of who she can be by identifying all of the potential services that the salon offers. Finally and most important, the stylist encourages the client to actualize her potential and go for it!

Can you think of a greater gift than your encouragement?

Measuring Your Encouraging Skills

Low Encouraging Skills	Medium Encouraging Skills	High Encouraging Skills
Rarely encourages clients client to try new looks; in fact, discourages clients who want more complicated or difficult treatments or cuts.	Encourages new clients to try new looks when they ask about them.	Encourages every to "Go for it!" and self-actualize their beauty potential.

Tips for Improving Your Encouragement Skills

1. Specialize: point out your client's hair potential and personality strengths.

2. Energize: share all the ideas you have for a great look – for her. You have so much to offer her to achieve an even better look.

3. Encourage her to "Go for it!"

If you've found these ideas meaningful, consider reading the book *The Skills of Encouragement* by Don Dinkmeyer and Lewis Losoncy.

Which Skill Is Being Used?

1) First Impression	__A. "Sounds like you feel very excited about a new look."
2) Bonding	__B. "That's amazing, we both went to Central High School!"
3) Empathizing	__C. "Just go for it, Mary!"
4) Specializing	

5) Energizing	__D. "I just learned this new style and I immediately thought of you."
6) Encouraging	__E. "Welcome to Stage Right, Mrs. James. I'm Melissa."
	__F. "Your hair has so many things going for it, Ginny. I love working with hair like yours!"

Answer:

3A, 2B, 6C, 4F, 1E, 5D

Applying Psy-Cosmetology to Touch People Sensitively at the 9 Service Points

Your technical skills demonstrate that you are an expert who can fulfill your client's cosmetic needs, your 7 Self-Motivation Strategies bring out your best attitude and optimism, and your 6 Person-Centered Skills build the relationship between you and your client. Now, your sensitive service skills will round out a perfect salon experience for your clients.

A Psy-Cosmetologist is able to:

- Project the ultimate service attitude in order to assure yourself professional fulfillment and prosperity.

- Use the 7 Self-Motivation Strategies: to Love Life, to be Driven from Within, to Change People's Lives, to be Open and Growing, to Highlight their Strengths, to Get over Stuff Quickly, and to Find a Way.

- Apply the 6 Person-Centered Skills covered earlier in the book: First Impression Skills, Bonding Skills, Empathizing Skills, Specializing Skills, Energizing Skills, and Encouraging Skills.

- Identify the 9 key Service Points in the total salon experience.

- Give service to people who will establish a loyalty with you.

- Remove every single point of "potential hassle" for the client in his or her salon experience.

- Turn a dissatisfied, complaining customer into a cheerleader for your salon. Service: The Other Side of the Cutting Edge

Albert Schweitzer asserted that "there is no higher religion than human service." Albert Einstein stated that "the only reason we are here on Earth is to be of service to one another." Alfred Adler, the noted psychiatrist of common sense, showed how serving others, or what he called "social interest," not only fulfills our need to contribute but exists at the very base of good mental health. Webster equates service with "usefulness," "benefits given to one another," or "a profession of respect communicated to another, like my service to you."

In his book *Earl Nightingale's Greatest Discovery*, Nightingale argues convincingly that our life, our income, and our respect are directly related to how well we serve other people's needs and wants. In their bestseller, *A Passion for Excellence*, Tom Peters and Nancy Austin devote five full chapters to the importance of service to customers, clients, or patience. And in Karl Albrecht and Ron Zemke's book *Service America*, the authors have more than two hundred pages of material to prove that the differential competitive edge for any business today is service. . . and it will be even more important tomorrow! Serve people's wants and needs well, and they will return. It's that simple! In fact, *Roget's Thesaurus* associates the word "service" with the word "value." I show how much I value you by how well I serve you. If I value you and serve you better than anyone else, you will become my client and stay my client. . . until the moment someone else starts to value you more by providing better service than I do.

In his classic book *The Magic of Thinking Big,* David Schwartz concludes on the topic of service, "The seed of money is service. Put service first and money takes care of itself. Always give people more than they expect to get. Each little extra thing you do for others is a money seed."

At this moment you are making a commitment either to mediocrity or to excellence in service. Your future as a salon professional rests on this decision. You can do it!

This chapter on service is the most important part of this book. Here we will look at how people sense a business's service attitude, how salon service can be measured, evaluated, and improved, and – most important – what you can do specifically at every Service Point in your salon to provide a positive, enriching, and memorable experience for your clients! Service is the other side of the cutting edge.

Positive Service Attitude: Sensing the Service Attitude of a Business

In one restaurant, the service attitude of the business is reflected by a waitress who gets snappy at a customer because he requests a special order. The menu is full of stern phrases like "absolutely no substitutes." In another restaurant only a few doors away, the customers are encouraged not to limit themselves by the menu but to think about what they are in the mood to eat. This restaurant, its employees, and its chef take enthusiastic pride in customer satisfaction. Good service starts with customer needs and wants, not restaurant workers' or chefs' egos. Remember Rule #1 – The Customer Is Always Right. This restaurant is service- sensitive, and its staff realizes that while in most of their lives they are "receivers" of services and can demand, in this instance they are the "givers" of a service and now have to demand the best in themselves. You as a customer can sense the difference in service attitude very clearly, and in the future you will vote by selecting the restaurant that acted with a positive service attitude that respected customers.

Contrasting Two Salons' Service Attitudes

SALON A. Clients enter with no one to greet them, are unsure where to put their coats, and sit in a dirty reception area, bored, waiting for service. The stylist takes personal phone calls on their time, talks about other clients, and offers them no new ideas on hairstyles or home care.

SALON B. Clients walk into a bright, cheerful environment where they get a friendly "Hello" from the receptionist or another staff member that seems to say, "I'm glad to see you." (Here is an example of the Specializing Skill, communicating that you are a unique person and we are looking forward to serving you.)

That special person, the client, waits in a clean reception area with books and magazines depicting many different styles she could choose. (Here is an example of Energizing Skills to get her excited about new looks.)

She is reassured by a staff member that her wait will be brief and is even offered a cup of coffee or tea. (This staff member is appealing to the client's senses of taste and smell while communicating that the salon knows her time is valuable.)

Her stylist soon arrives giving off warm First Impression skills, and connects with the client auditorily, tactilely, and visually.

The stylist accompanies her to the first service while sensing opportunities to use her Bonding Skills by finding commonalities.

She then uses her Empathy Skills to sense the client's feelings during the consultation. She again uses her Specializing Skills when she's pointing out the client's positive features and hair, skin and nail potential.

When sharing new styles, texture treatments, and colors, she can hardly contain her excitement – this stylist really has Energizing Skills.

Sensing the client's desire to take full advantage of the salon's benefits, the stylist uses her Encouraging Skills to motivate the client to go for whatever new look is most exciting to her.

Throughout the process, the stylist is getting her client excited about a professional program of caring for her hair at home between appointments.

Over a period of time, which salon will be booming with clients? Again, the answer is obvious – the salon with the sensitive service skills!

It's possible to observe, measure, and improve a salon's service attitude. Consider this Service-Attitude Rating Scale:

LOW SERVICE ATTITUDE: Client viewed as an annoyance, made to apologize for any need or want she has, e.g., wants to talk about straightening but the stylist rushes through the service, or needs to go to the bathroom but feels too intimidated to say so. No staff member smiles and client is ignored by stylists joking with each other.

MEDIUM-LOW SERVICE ATTITUDE: Client viewed with a tolerance, a necessary evil. Staff sees her as a number, a head. She probably will not ask for additional services but if she does, she will apologize.

MEDIUM SERVICE ATTITUDE: Treatment of client neither significantly positive or negative. Salon gives client what she says she wants, no more, no less. If client asks for additional services, the salon will comply.

MEDIUM-HIGH SERVICE ATTITUDE: Salon team talks about the importance of servicing client's needs. All staff is sensitive, but salon has no established plan for all of the sensitive Service Points in the client's salon experience.

HIGH SERVICE SUPERIORITY: Salon team has a formal plan to ensure client comfort and convenience at every Service Point. Pride of service is felt by the total team. Staff members use all six person-centered skills.

We have discussed the importance of good service and establishing a positive service attitude. We then listed a system to evaluate a salon's service attitude from a low to a high level. The biggest difference involved HAVING A FORMAL PLAN at every sensitive Service Point in the client's total salon experience. What are the 9 key sensitive Service Points?

1) Salon Contact

2) Salon Entry

3) Reception Area and Pre-Service

4) Consultation

5) Shampooing

6) Technical Services and Recommendation

7) Client Reaction and Feedback from Services

8) Remuneration for Services

9) Staff-supported client "debut"

Considering each of these Service Points, how can a salon create an atmosphere that guarantees a positive experience for every client, thus assuring success?

Let's study each Service Point separately and offer some suggestions to streamline salon service. You will then be encouraged to add any of your own service-sensitive ideas at each key point. We will study each Service Point by contrasting a low service attitude with a high service attitude.

Service Point 1: Salon Contact

The client's direct contact with the salon is either salon- or client-initiated. Many more progressive salons are not waiting passively for people to seek out their services but HAVE AN ACTIVE PLAN to initiate contact with clients.

However, most salons place the responsibility for salon contact on the client. A person's direct contact with the salon occurs in three ways: either by walking in, telephoning the salon for an appointment, or making an appointment on-line. Let's consider service to the client who contacts the salon for an appointment.

We'll contrast the low-service salon with the high-service salon and see how they treat the client at this Service Point.

Low Salon Service	High Salon Service
Long wait before the phone is answered; harsh, discourteous response.	Prompt response; pleasantly answered, enthusiastic tone.
Receives a reservation from a client on-line and offers no response in return.	Receives a reservation from a client on-line and confirms and reassures through a return call that the time slot will be reserved for them.
Dull voice giving client vibes that salon couldn't care less.	Receptionist's voice gives feeling, "Glad you called, excited to hear from you."
Ignores name of client; doesn't introduce self.	Uses client's name frequently; makes sure client knows stylist by name.
Cold, just-the-facts kind of treatment.	Builds anticipation about the salon, the staff, and the benefits; gets client excited about visit; says something special about stylist serving client.
Poor English or curt manner, e.g., "What do you want?"	Clearly articulated communications, e.g., "How may we be of service to you?"

Hearing the client's voice on the phone has the advantage of sensing any concerns or questions she might have. Take advantage of applying some of the six person-centered skills in this first contact over the phone:

First Impression Skills – The phone call is limited to auditory contact, and research indicates that the talker's smile can be sensed over the phone. A smile when receiving that first reservation call from a client is an ideal situation to make a cheerful, reassuring first impression.

Bonding Skills – The sensitive salon employee taking a call listens both for areas of agreement and cues to the client's personality. For example, if the caller says, "I like morning appointments - can I see you tomorrow morning?" the staff member might respond, "Absolutely. I'm an early riser myself (Areas of Agreement). We'll be looking for you early tomorrow (Connecting to the caller's visual style).

Empathizing Skills – The salon employee listens for the feelings of the caller and echoes the sentiments back. "Sounds like you're really excited about trying out a new look!"

Energizing Skills – (Getting the caller energized for the visit) "Our staff is known for their outstanding color services. Your stylist Jen will be able to explore many possibilities with you!"

Encouraging Skills – "Start dreaming about some ideas you have. We are looking forward to seeing you in the morning!"

Salon contact, as you can see, is a vital Service Point because it sets the stage in the client's mind about the attitude of the salon. Salons report that sometimes first-time clients who call in to make an appointment do not show. In 90 percent of these cases, the reason is that the salon failed at this first Service Point.

Psychologically, people conclude that the attitudes and vibes they perceive in the person they speak to initially represent those of the total salon. Feel free to add any additional suggestions that a salon could use to improve its service at Service Point 1, salon contact:

_____

_____

_____

_____

_____

_____

_____

Now let's consider how we can improve at the next step.

Service Point 2: Salon Entry

As the saying goes, "There's no second chance to make a first impression."
A person experiences their first visual impression as they enter the salon.
Psychologist B.F. Skinner reveals how we can use behavior modification to
reward a person when he exhibits desirable behavior. Certainly a client's
entry into a salon is desirable for that salon and needs to be rewarded or
reinforced by a staff member's attention. Reinforcing a client's entry into the
salon can be done with a smile, a touch, food, coupons, compliments and a
clean, attractive environment. Skinner's experiments showed that what was
reinforced tended to occur again if reinforcement occurred immediately after
the desirable action, ideally within a few seconds. Obviously a salon full of
Psy-Cosmetologists is reinforcing, because they are lovers of life and they
loving changing people's lives. What could create a better first impression than
a business full of self-starting stylists who are enthusiastic about bettering
themselves and others? The team is alive, and when the people in the salon are
alive, the salon itself is alive.

To enhance its chances of having a client return, the salon can reinforce
that client's entry. In other words, it is important for people to feel welcome,
recognized, and reinforced (rewarded) at this Service Point. It is also vital that
the client feel "good vibes" from the total salon environment.

Let's observe the differences between low and high service ratings:

Low Salon Service

No one to greet client at entry,
or client ignored.

No directions given; client feels
anxiety about how to act and
what to do.

Client senses cold "people
atmosphere,"tension among staff.

Upon entry, client immediately
senses cold physical environment
without ambience.

Client is responsible for making
herself at home.

High Salon Service

Client immediately acknowledged with
a cheerful welcome.

Client is invited into reception area,
assisted with coat, and offered
reassurance.

Warm smiles, friendly attitudes, and
harmony in salon help client relax.

Upon entry, client sees attractive salon
colors; cleanliness, the right music for
the clientele. Staff appearance suggest
both sensitivity and professionalism.

Salon staff takes responsibility to help
this client feel as comfortable as she
can.

Add any suggestions of your own to provide better service at the point where the client enters the salon:

_____

_____

_____

_____

_____

_____

_____

_____

Service Point 3: Salon Reception Area and Pre-Service Experiences

The salon's most underestimated area of potential for service is the reception area. A client waits, often bored, with little to do. She stares at the walls, looks at other people, or reads a magazine. Some salons have been studying this area to help people spend this time usefully. Perhaps clients could learn more about the salon – pictures, biographies, or styles done by its professional staff – and the benefits the salon has to offer. A professionally made retail display can energize a client's interest in home hair care. (Notice that Energizing Skills can be employed in the salon even without a stylist present.) (Also, Encouragement Skills can be used in the words, "Go for it!" when talking about professional products for home use.)

It is true that most delays are the fault of clients who are late; nevertheless, dealing with the waiting time of punctual clients is the salon's responsibility. When it is obvious that a certain stylist is running significantly late, the sensitive salon will call the following clients and inform them of the delay. Most people have things they would rather do than wait in the reception area.

Let's contrast the low- and high-service salons in their ways of approaching service in the reception area:

Low Salon Service

Client just waits.

High Salon Service

Receptionist uses Specializing Skills by pointing out something positive about the client's appearance, dress or personality. Receptionist uses Bonding Skills by finding similarities between the client and the stylist who will be seeing her.

Low Salon Service	High Salon Service
Client just waits.	The nail technician or skin-care specialist uses Energizing Skills by demonstrating to the client how to care for skin or nails. Client sees additional services salon offers.
Client just waits.	A stylist who is free at the time takes a few minutes to share some ideas about home hair-care products or other services of the salon.
Client just waits.	Client watches videos related to hairstyle and lifestyle.
Client just waits.	Salon gives client brochure on the relationship between appearance and success on the job, appearance and popularity. This offers additional value to the salon services and products.
Client just waits – another one joins in the wait.	Receptionist shares with the client the salon's new promotion program giving a free cut for every two promotions she refers.
Clients just wait, occasionally glancing at each other.	Receptionist starts to excite the client by telling her about the special skills her stylist has, e.g., texture treatments. "Have you ever had a body wave? I'd think you'd look great!"
Clients form Salon Client Waiters' Club.	A free hair-color consultation is given to the client.
Client leaves area to get her service.	Client leaves reception area inquiring if it is possible to get both color and a perm in the same appointment and if the salon's client-referral program can be used more than once.
Client forgotten about.	Client receives e-mail from salon during the week with staff apologies for the delay. Salon knows she is a busy woman. Referral system's rules changed only for her – one for one!

Service Point 4: Consultation

The professional cosmetologist or stylist is an expert in hair cutting, coloring, texturing, home care, and everything else that relates to the cosmetic improvement of the client. The study of Psy-Cosmetology assists the professional stylist in communicating more effectively with clients through Empathizing Skills and the other skills we address in this book. The Psy-Cosmetologist focuses on the importance of a client's self-image, both inner and outer. Everything points to one fact: a cosmetologist, especially one who has taken time to study people, is in an excellent position to serve as a consultant of hair, image, and matching hairstyle to a client's lifestyle.

From our perspective, the best time for the Service Point of consultation to occur is prior to the shampooing. The reason is this – the stylist is seeing the client in a natural state, not with shampooed hair. And, of course, the more accurate the information a stylist has about a person, the more effective her advice can be. When you are giving a consultation, you are probably doing what only five percent of what stylists do. Consultation is a necessary part of every Psy-Cosmetologist's work.

There is one thing that every Psy-Cosmetologist agrees on – consultation is a vital, necessary point of his or her work. Consultation builds client loyalty because it obviously shows that the stylist cares and is interested in providing the best possible service for clients.

Gifts the Client Brings to the Consultation

The most rewarding consultations allow both stylist and client the experience of communicating and sharing beneficial thoughts and ideas. In that special communication, both people work hard to unwrap the gift the other brings to the professional relationship.

The client's contribution to the relationship is her LIFESTYLE – that is, the "total person," including past experiences, present self-image, and visions of who she can be. Lifestyle comprises the total self – self as a member of a family, as part of a neighborhood, community, city, state, or society; self as part of a career, workforce, or profession; self as an earner with a certain income and financial worth; self as a spiritual member of a religion; self with certain values of life that are uncompromising; self as athletic or not; and a view of self as an attractive or unattractive person. There are no limits to the complex human being awaiting service in the stylist's chair. WHAT A CLIENT BRINGS TO THE SALON IS A COMPLEX THING CALLED LIFESTYLE. This is her gift to the client-stylist relationship.

Gifts the Stylist Brings to the Consultation

Now, let's look at what the professional cosmetologist offers in meeting the LIFESTYLE of the client. The stylist's Empathizing Skills are the most important tool to help the stylist understand the person's feelings and lifestyle. By understanding a person's lifestyle, the stylist can use her Specializing Skills to identify the unique and total person of the client. The stylist brings a creative talent to help someone look and feel her best: skills in cutting, coloring, perming, and manicuring, and recommendations to help the client maximize her appearance. The stylist brings awareness of all of the benefits a client can receive from the salon, a knowledge of trends and new directions in hair, day-in and day-out experience in designing people's appearances. THE STYLIST'S GIFTS TO THE RELATIONSHIP ARE KNOWLEDGE AND CREATIVITY FOR THE CLIENT'S MAXIMUM BENEFIT. The stylist's gifts are enhanced through their Bonding, Empathizing, Specializing, Energizing, and Encouraging Skills.

The difference between low salon service and high salon service at Service Point 4 is simply this – the high-service salon HAS A PLAN and offers consultation initiated by the stylist with every client, except in the case of standing weekly appointments.

Contrast the low-, the medium-, and the high-service salon on consultation:

Low Salon Service	Medium Salon Service	High Salon Service
No consultation.	Consultation given when requested.	Consultation offered to every client.

Add suggestions or thoughts that you have to improve service at the consultation Service Point:

_____

_____

_____

_____

_____

_____

_____

_____

Service Point 5: Shampooing

When a client moves from the consultation area to the shampooing area, is she accompanied by someone and properly introduced or is she simply told to go there? Let's contrast the low- and high-service salon in terms of their service attitude toward the client in the shampooing area:

Low Salon Service

No psychological contact before physical contact with client's hair.

Shampoo technician provides no information about the service she is providing and believes that all she needs to do is shampoo the hair.

Shampoo technician takes personal calls on client's time.

Shampoo technician inconsiderate of client by not being concerned about the client's comfort.

Shampoo technician sees self as isolated from the other stylists. Does not work as part of the team.

High Salon Service

Shampoo technician makes psychological contact with First Impression Skills with an introduction, referring to client by name, a smile, and a handshake.

Shampoo technician sees self as an expert in hair care who has more information than the client on how to do it. As a Psy- Cosmetologist, a Shampoo Technician highlights her strengths and acts like the valuable member of the team she is. Shampoo person sees herself as an educator and takes pride in product knowledge. She uses her Energizing Skills to show client step-by-step ways to care for her own hair. She encourages her client to use the professional products that are perfect for the client's specialized needs.

Salon professional, sensitive to service and client's needs, shows respect by telling receptionist, "I can't take that call now; I'm with Mrs. G."

Person shampooing hair uses her Empathizing Skills by seeking the client's feelings on water temperature and pressure applied during manipulation.

Shampoo technician uses Energizing Skills and helps client feel excited about going to the next Service Point, the styling area.

Add any suggestions in order to service a client more sensitively in the shampoo area:

_____

_____

_____

_____

_____

_____

_____

_____

Service Point 6: Technical Services and Recommendations

The actual technical service is the meat of the whole salon experience. As a meal is the reason one goes to a restaurant, cut, color, or treatment is the reason a client goes to a salon. The other Service Points are not the dinner, but they are the background music that makes the dinner more enjoyable – the candle on the table to bring the right atmosphere, the bottle of champagne, the friendly waitress, the chef who comes to your table. You can go to a restaurant and have "something to eat," or you can have "a dining experience" designed around your own needs to relax and feel comfortable, recognized, and important. All indicators are that the average person will pay more for that.

The high-service salon spends time carefully assessing the client's expectations and clarifying them to make sure they are shared and mutually agreed upon. The excellent salon has stylist who are sensitive to body language, especially facial expressions, at every step of the process. In cases where the client is experiencing new services, the ultimate salon makes sure its professionals reassure her if she is unaware of how the procedures work. The winning salon respects and doesn't intimidate clients or discourage questions. It realizes full well that the average person hasn't taken 1,500 to 2,500 hours in beauty school.

Contrast the difference between the low- and high-service salon and stylist during the technical Service Point:

Low Salon Service	High Salon Service
Lack of attention to client. Continually walks away.	Immersed in service. Shows client she is special; refuses phone calls of a personal nature. Stylist uses Specializing Skills to convey how much she enjoys being with her client. "I love working with your hair!"

Low Salon Service	High Salon Service
Just gives service without explaining.	Uses Empathizing Skills by sensing client's feelings, anxieties, uncertainties. Takes the mystery out of the process by sharing with client what she is doing from time to time.
Apathetic to client inconveniences.	Uses Empathizing Skills by being sensitive to client comfort, e.g., avoids dripping perm solution, itching cut hair on neck, color stains on skin.
Client not informed when service finished; feels stupid about salon etiquette.	Good-communicating stylist escorts client to the next Service Point, using Bonding Skills to keep in agreement mode.

Add your suggestions to improve technical services or recommendations in the salon:

_____

_____

_____

_____

_____

_____

_____

_____

Service Point 7: Client Reaction and Feedback from Services

The stylist pulled the cape off the client's shoulders, glanced briefly at her, asked "What do you think?" without waiting for an answer, and looked for the next client. The client experienced a stylist who wasn't honestly interested in what she really thought. The stylist was functioning on automatic pilot as it is so easy to do under the demands and stresses of the average day in a busy salon. The client is more aware of the treatment than the stylist is.

It's easy to ask for client reactions to services: The hard part is to really listen – but not for the Psy-Cosmetologist! As you may recall from previous chapters, Psy-Cosmetologists are open and growing, they get over stuff quickly, and they find away. The Psy-Cosmetologist takes negative feedback as a learning opportunity because it allows her to correct any problems and thus improve. Do you remember the Johari Window? Getting feedback from another person can open up our "blind area." Remember – the Psy-Cosmetologist is a criticism welcomer. Plus, stylists who encourage feedback, especially from dissatisfied people, are in touch with what the research has found on success in business.

"Hey, We Haven't Seen Emily in a While"

Studies demonstrate the importance of creating an atmosphere where people feel safe and are encouraged to voice their dissatisfaction. Some eye-opening findings on handling dissatisfied customers and creating systems to get feedback are the following:

• The average business never hears from ninety-six percent of its unhappy customers. For every complaint received, the average is in fact twenty-six customers with problems, six of which are "serious" problems.

• Complainers are more likely than non-complainers to do business again with the company that upset them, even if the problem isn't satisfactorily resolved.

• Of the customers who register complaints, between fifty-four and seventy percent will do business again with the organization if their complaints are resolved. That figure goes up to a staggering ninety-five percent if customers feel that the complaints were resolved quickly.

• The average customer who has a problem with an organization tells nine or ten people about it. Thirteen percent of people who have a problem with an organization recount the incident to more than twenty people.

• Customers who have complained to an organization and had their complaints satisfactorily resolved tell an average of five people about the treatment they received.

What does all this tell the service-oriented salon? First, just because someone doesn't tell the salon that she was dissatisfied doesn't mean she was satisfied, because ninety-six percent never share their complaints. The horror-show about this is that even if they do not complain to you, they may be sharing their negative experiences through reviews on-line. A simple rule of thumb is this – if they don't share it with you, they're going to share it with the community.

Second, a salon needs to have a sensitive system that encourages a dissatisfied person to feel comfortable discussing her concern. What we have found is that the more Empathizing Skills a stylist has to understand the client's feelings, the more willing the client is to share their feedback.

Third, the salon can keep that client by making every effort to assuage her dissatisfaction. The Psy-Cosmetologist is trained to find a way and believe that every challenge has a solution.

Fourth, the business value of one client is in that client's word-of-mouth effect on the salon. Seek out, find, and service the dissatisfied clients. Success is yours! Perhaps the greatest benefit of being a Psy-Cosmetologist is in the area of dealing with challenges.

The high-service team knows the facts that lie deep within this research. Success or failure today depends upon three things:

1. Satisfying people's wants and needs (Empathizing Skills).
2. Creating a system by which they can feel safe to share their feelings (Empathizing Skills).
3. Responding to their feedback (Finding a way).

The low-service salon doesn't encourage feedback and client reaction, either out of inflated ego or lack of confidence (which underneath are the same), or doesn't really listen to client feedback. In either case it ignores the facts, the research, and sadly. . . its own future.

Opportunity Is Knocking for a Stylist Who Doesn't Intimidate

I have never seen a greater time for opportunity for any salon than today – that is, for a people-oriented salon. When I was on some call-in radio and TV talk shows, almost every caller expressed the same concern about feeling afraid or intimidated by her stylist. In most cases he or she chose to leave that stylist and find a more service-oriented one. Many others expressed a desire to go to another stylist in the same salon but didn't want to upset their current stylist.

This is a time of prosperity for any stylist who has the courage to seek out honest reactions from people at this seventh and very important Service Point in the salon experience.

Low Salon Service	High Salon Service
Doesn't ask how client likes the service or asks and does not listen.	Realizes that the most important reason the client comes is to look and feel better, and finding out if the client is satisfied is the vital question.

Add any additional suggestions to improve the client's willingness to be honest and share his or her reactions to the technical services:

_____

_____

_____

_____

_____

_____

_____

_____

Service Point 8: Payment for Services

Roget's Thesaurus equates renumeration or payment with "reward." The client who is paying for the services she receives in the salon is the reward the salon owner gets for establishing a business and the staff gets for providing services. As an individual who is driven from within and highlights her own strengths, a Psy-Cosmetologist understands that payment is the result of a fulfilling job well done and a satisfied customer. The reward is just as much having a happy returning client as receiving a single paycheck or a tip.

Some stylists are almost apologetic or defensive about asking a client for payment. These stylists forget that the service they have to offer is one by which they help a client look and feel good. They should be proud to be rewarded for fine service. Why?

It's very simple. For the client's sake. A client who has been extremely satisfied by excellent service in a high-service salon wants to see that salon stay in business. She wants her stylist to stay successful so she can in the future continue to have her wants and needs satisfied. For that salon to remain in business, there must be a payment (and if a salon is a low-service salon and isn't service-oriented, do you think a client would have the same attitude toward it?)

Notice the difference between low salon service and high salon service at the payment Service Point:

Low Salon Service	High Salon Service
Hands client the check and allows her to return to the reception area alone to wait for someone to take her money.	Escorts client to the reception area where the stylist/receptionist reassures her that she made the right decision.
Allows client to leave salon without recommending proper home hair-care maintenance.	Makes sure that proper home hair-care products are recommended so client can get the most out of her investment.
Works on a "cash only" basis.	Makes many different modes of payment available to client.
Asks client to pay up front so that the receptionist may leave early.	Receptionist stays in salon until the last client has left.

Add your suggestions to provide better service at the payment Service Point:

_____

_____

_____

_____

_____

Service Point 9: Staff-Supported Client "Debut"

We talked about the power of first impressions, but there is also the power of last impressions – Service Point 9 – in which the salon shows its interest and continued support of the client as she makes her debut with her new style or color. In these cases where the client has had the courage to change styles (with the help of the stylist's Encouraging Skills), it is especially important that the salon support her decision and communicate its further support for her until the next appointment. She must know the staff is behind her.

Contrast the difference between low salon support and high salon support:

Low Salon Support	High Salon Support
Allows client to depart without any comment on her appearance, leaving client with the feeling, "Why did I spend the extra money if the salon didn't even see the difference?"	Using Specializing Skills, compliments some aspect of the client's hair, skin or nails that has been impacted by treatment in the salon.
Salon staff assumes client has the tools, the skills, and the knowledge to care for her hair at home.	Salon professional further reinforces or rewards the client's need for home hair-care enhancement support by using Energizing Skills to recommend the best tools, products, and knowledge to care for hair (if stylist forgot).
Staff allows client to leave without a plan for continuing the relationship.	Salon shows support and interest in the client by Energizing the client for the next appointment. Salon calls client in the interim using Empathizing Skills if client either seemed a little uncertain during the feedback service or received a new service.

In a high staff-supported client debut, the client feels newfound confidence in her relationship with a service oriented-salon of professional cosmetologists who stand beside her and support her needs. That is the ultimate in service! The salon has given her a guarantee of a long-term relationship, which means she doesn't have to go through the consultation process again somewhere else, with someone she doesn't know. Her search is over! That's something a low-service salon just wouldn't do.

Add any suggestions you can for providing sensitive ways to help clients feel supported by your salon team members when clients debut with a new style:

_____

_____

_____

_____

_____

_____

_____

You have just experienced a rigorous, psychologically-based service-sensitive professional development program for salon professionals. At times you may have been overwhelmed with how complex doing a "good job" seems. But it's actually not. You see, each of the points in this chapter reflects the ideal, not the typical. There are very few, if any, salons in the world that are totally and completely high-service all the time, good days and bad. These ideas are designed to get you thinking about a plan for providing better service.

You have your technical tools for styling. Now you have acquired your motivational and person-centered styling skills to compliment those technical skills. Look at what tools the Psy-Cosmetologist has at these 9 Service Points:

Psy-Cosmetologists:

- Love life
- Are driven from within
- Change people's lives
- Are open and growing
- Highlight their strengths
- Get over stuff quickly
- Find a way

Psy-Cosmetologists:

- Greet people warmly (First impression Skills)
- Connect with people (Bonding Skills)
- Sense feelings (Empathizing Skills)
- Experience everyone as important (Specializing Skills)
- Are excited about their professional gifts (Energizing Skills)
- Inspire a "Go For It!" feeling (Encouragement Skills)

Putting on the Final Touches

Congratulations! We have come a long way together. I hope you have grown on our journey to understanding the beauty in people and the beauty in your work. Now put the final touches on yourself as a Psy-Cosmetologist to experience your new professional insights.

You learned that:

You touch people, are with them during every emotional moment of their life, and have the **people** and **technical** skills to make people **feel** and **be** beautiful.

You are **alive,** are **driven from within, change people's lives, are open to grow, can highlight your strengths, get over stuff quickl**y and **find a way** to achieve your clients' and your own dreams.

You have acquired the skills to make a great **first impression**, to **connect** with people, to **empathize** and understand a person's feelings, to make any person you meet feel special, can **energize** people to realize all your salon has to offer, and to **encourage** people to go for being nothing less than their best.

I believe you have never been more ready to do your important work – the work of a Psy-Cosmetologist, of the beauty in people, and of a "bringing it on" feeling.

Love

Dr. Lew

For any questions, further dialogue, or challenges with material in this chapter, please email us at howardh@peoplemediainc.com.

Psy-Cosmetology Terminology

Agreement Skills: The ability to get people into an agreement mode.

Attitude toolbox: The combination of our thoughts, our emotions and our actions, which together form our attitude.

Attraction-reciprocation effect: The more a client feels a stylist likes them, the more they will like the stylist. One of the Psy-Cosmetologist's laws of service sensibility.

Auditory bias: A tendency to experience the world through spoken words and sounds.

Benefits-interest effect: The more benefits a client feels a stylist has that they want, the more they will listen to what the stylist has to say. One of the Psy-Cosmetologist's laws of service sensibility.

Bonding Skills: The ability to make connections with all kinds of people.

Consistency-trust effect: The more a stylist is consistent with the client, the more the client will trust you. One of the Psy-Cosmetologist's laws of service sensibility.

Criticism welcomer: A person who listens to criticism with the desire to improve and the ability to ignore insults.

Emotional Labor: The energy you exert on caring for a client.

Empathizing Skills: The ability to understand another person's feelings and communicate them back to the person.

Encouragement-excitement Effect: The more a client is encouraged to grow and try new things, the more the stylist-client relationship will remain fresh. One of the Psy-Cosmetologist's laws of service sensibility.

Encouragement Skills: The ability to provide conditions to bring out the courage of your clients to grow.

Energizing Skills: The ability to get people excited about all of the professional benefits available in the salon.

Enthusiasm-bigger goals effect: The more enthused a stylist is about a client's possibilities, the more the client will see new potential in themselves. One of the Psy-Cosmetologist's laws of service sensibility.

First Impression Skills: The ability to give off positive vibes to help others feel welcomed and safe.

Flow: The experience of finding deeper or higher meaning in any experience and is more mental than the more sensual state of being mindful

Growth-centered: The mindset of people who are open to new ideas because of the promise of self-improvement.

Growth decision: The decision that occurs when we make the decisions to go out of our comfort zone in order to improve ourselves.

Holistic view: The experience of looking at all factors to get a fuller understanding of a situation.

Human revolution: The movement occurring in society in which the consumer is increasingly aware of its power to choose where they spend their money.

Important-reciprocation Effect: The more important a client feels, the more successful a client will help a stylist become. One of the Psy-Cosmetologist's laws of service sensibility.

Inner drive: The experience of being motivated from within.

Johari window: A technique to measure one's self-awareness.

Mindfulness: A fuller awareness of our present experience with acceptance.

Non-verbal communication: How people communicate, intentionally and unintentionally, without words.

Problem resolution-loyalty effect: The more hair problems a stylist solves, the more loyalty a client will feel to them. One of the Psy-Cosmetologist's laws of service sensibility.

Psy-Cosmetology: The blending of the sciences of psychology and cosmetology.

REACH concept: Relating through Emphasizing the Assets in the Client's Hair.

Self-actualizing: Maslow's term for those who are bringing out their fuller potential.

Sensory representational style: The way we represent the world to ourselves.

Similarity-comfort effect: The more a client feels a stylist is similar to them, the more a client will feel they know the stylist. One of the Psy-Cosmetologist's laws of service sensibility.

Specializing Skills: The ability to help another person to feel unique in a positive way.

Subconscious mind: The achieving, doing mind that follows the directions of the conscious, directing mind.

Tactile bias: A tendency to approach the world through words that highlight textures and physical contact.

Technical labor: The energy you exert on styles, colors and professional recommendations for a client.

Understanding needs-satisfaction effect: The more a stylist listens to a client's unique needs, the more information a stylist will have about the client's likes and dislikes. One of the Psy-Cosmetologist's laws of service sensibility.

Uniqueness-attention effect: The more a stylist customizes their approach to a client's likes and dislikes, the more a stylist's methods will catch the client's attention. One of the Psy-Cosmetologist's laws of service sensibility.

Visual bias: A tendency to respond to words that create images, sights and pictures.

"We" references: Making statements that communicate that you and your client feel the same way about something.

"Yes" mood: A tone of agreement created by talking about the other person's interests and by asking questions that are likely to elicit "yes" answers.

Bibliography

Adler, Alfred. *Social Interest*. New York: Putnam, 1939.

Adler, Alfred. *Understanding Human Nature*. New York: Greenberg, 1927.

Akert, Robin M., Eliot Aronson and Timothy D. Wilson. *Social Psychology*. Upper Saddle River, NJ: Pearson Education, Inc., 2007.

Alberti, Robert E. and Michael Emmons. *Your Perfect Right*. San Luis Obispo: Impact, 1982.

Albrecht, Karl and Ron Zemke. *Service America: Doing Business in the New Economy*. Homewood, IL: Dow-Jones Irwin, 1985.

Brim, Brian and Tony Rutigliano. *Strengths Based Selling*. New York: Gallup Press, 2010.

Brooks, Michael. *Instant Rapport*. New York: Grand Central Publishing, 1989.

Carlzon, Jan. *Moments of Truth*. Cambridge, MA: Bellinger, 1987.

Dinkmeyer, Don and Lewis Losoncy. *The Encouragement Book: On Becoming a Positive Person*. Englewood Cliffs: Prentice, 1980.

Dinkmeyer, Don and Lewis Losoncy. *The Skills of Encouragement*. Boca Raton, FL: St. Lucie Press, 1996.

Ellis, Albert. *Reason and Emotion in Psychotherapy*. Secaucus, NJ: Lyle Stuart, 1962.

Ellis, Albert and Robert Harper. *A New Guide to Rational Living*. North Hollywood: Wilshire Book Company, 1975.

Fulton, Paul R., Christopher K. Germer and Ronald D. Siegel, eds. *Mindfulness and Psychotherapy*. New York: The Guilford Press, 2005.

Graham, Jean Ann and Albert M. Kligman. *The Psychology of Cosmetic Treatments*. New York: Praeger Publishers, 1985.

Hogan, Kevin. *The Psychology of Persuasion: How to Persuade Others to Your Way of Thinking*. Gretna, LA: Pelican Publishing Company, Inc, 1996.

"Impossible Doesn't Mean It Can't Be Done." *Matrix Business Builder*. Spring, 1987.

Irvine, William B. *A Guide to the Good Life*. New York: Oxford University Press, 2009.

Lazarus, Arnold and Bernie Zilbergeld. *Mind Power*. New York: Little, 1987.

Lobsenz, Norman M. and Henfrie Weisinger. *Nobody's Perfect*. New York: Warner, 1981.

Losoncy, Lewis and Dennis McClellan. *Early Poppers: Secrets of Self-Starters*. Sanford, FL: DC Press, 2010.

Losoncy, Lewis. *If It Weren't For the Customer, Selling Would Be Easy!* Sanford, FL: DC Press, 2006.

Losoncy, Lewis and Colin Walsh. *On: A Brilliant Way to Live & Work.* Sanford, FL: DC Press, 2011.

Losoncy, Lewis and Joe Santy. *Passionate Salon Professionals.* Sanford, FL: DC Press, 2007.

Losoncy, Lewis and Donald W. Scoleri. *The New Psy-Cosmetologist.* Reading, PA: People-Media, Inc, 1990.

Losoncy, Lewis. *Think Your Way to Success.* North Hollywood, CA: Wilshire Book Company, 1983.

Losoncy, Lewis. *Today! Grab It: 7 Vital Attitude Nutrients to Build the New You.* Boca Raton, FL: St. Lucie Press, 1998.

Losoncy, Lewis. *Turning People On: How to Be an Encouraging Person.* Englewood Cliffs: Prentice, 1977.

Losoncy, Lewis. *You Can Do It: How to Encourage Yourself.* Englewood Cliffs: Prentice, 1980.

Maltz, Maxwell. *Psycho-Cybernetics.* North Hollywood: Wilshire Book Company, 1960.

Maslow, Abraham. *The Farther Reaches of Human Nature.* New York: Viking, 1971.

Maslow, Abraham, ed. *Motivation and Personality.* New York: Harper, 1954.

Meherabian, Albert. *Non-Verbal Communication.* Chicago: Aldine-Atherton, 1972.

Montagu, Ashley. *Touching: The Human Significance of the Skin.* New York: Harper & Row, 1986.

Mortensen, Kurt W. *Maximum Influence.* New York: AMACOM, 2004.

Naisbitt, John. *Megatrends: Ten New Directions Transforming Our Lives.* New York: Warner, 1982.

Nightingale, Earl. *Earl Nightingale's Greatest Discovery.* New York: Mead, 1987.

Peters, Tom and Nancy Austin. *A Passion for Excellence: Leadership Difference.* New York: Random, 1985.

Peters, Tom and Robert Waterman. *In Search of Excellence: Lessons from America's Best-Run Companies.* New York: Warner, 1984.

Rogers, Carl R. *On Becoming a Person.* Boston: Houghton, 1961.

Schwartz, David. *The Magic of Thinking Big.* North Hollywood: Wilshire Book Company, 1962.

About the Author

Lewis Losoncy, "Dr. Lew," has inspired hairdressers world-wide for the last three decades. He is the author of 26 books on motivation, encouragement, positive attitude, leadership and teamwork.

Never before has a psychologist made such a contribution to the vibrancy and business of beauty as Dr. Losoncy has done. He has transported the psychological importance of "beauty" to the minds of the world. Not only has he enhanced the way the public views their hairstylist, but as importantly, he has enhanced the hairstylists' own value of self.

From his groundbreaking book, first published in 1985, *The New Psy-Cosmetologist*, Dr. Losoncy has built a foundation "making hairstylists aware that what they are really offering for their clients is not just a haircut, but rather CONFIDENCE" – that psychological kick that one gets from going to the salon so vital to their personal happiness.

To the general public he is known as "The Doctor of Encouragement." To the beauty profession he would like to be known as their friend.

Become a

PSY-COSMETOLOGIST

ORDERING INFORMATION

To order additional *On Becoming a Psy-Cosmetologist* books, workbooks for in-salon staff meetings, teachers' manuals or Psy-Cosmetologist merchandise, please visit our website at
www.psy-cosmetology.com
or email
orders@psy-cosmetology.com
for more information about placing orders.

EDUCATIONAL OPPORTUNITIES

- Undergraduate student study
- online education
- locate a seminar near you

please visit our website at
www.psy-cosmetology.com
or email
education@psy-cosmetology.com

for more information regarding educational opportunities

Connect. Collaborate. Create.

If you've enjoyed your experience

please let us know what you think and share with us how this book will help you in your personal and career goals.

To connect with other like-minded professionals,
please visit our website blog at
www.psy-cosmetology.com

Follow us on: